P9-CPX-357

WILLIAM HUTT
Masks and Faces

KEITH GAREBIAN
EDITOR

WILLIAM HUTT
Masks and Faces

KEITH GAREBIAN
EDITOR

Mosaic Press
Oakville, On. - Buffalo, N.Y.

Canadian Cataloguing in Publication Data

Main entry under title:

William Hutt

Includes index.
ISBN 0-88962-583-2

1. Huttt, William.   2. Actors - Canada - Biography.
I. Garebian, Keith, 1943-   .

PN2308.H87W5 1995   792'.092   C95-930664-1

No part of this book may be reproduced or transmitted in any form, by any means, electronic or mechanical, including photocopying and recording information storage and retrieval systems, without permission in writing from the publisher, except by a reviewer who may quote brief passages in a review.

Published by MOSAIC PRESS, P.O. Box 1032, Oakville, Ontario, L6J 5E9, Canada. Offices and warehouse at 1252 Speers Road, Units #1&2, Oakville, Ontario, L6L 5N9, Canada and Mosaic Press, 85 River Rock Drive, Suite 202, Buffalo, N.Y., 14207, USA.

Mosaic Press acknowledges the assistance of the Canada Council, the Ontario Arts Council, the Ontario Ministry of Culture, Tourism and Recreation and the Dept. of Communications, Government of Canada, for their support of our publishing programme.

Copyright © Keith Garebian 1995

Photograph: THE IMAGINARY INVALID Cylla von Tiedemann
Cover and book design by Susan Parker
Printed and bound in Canada
ISBN 0-88962-583-2

In Canada:
      MOSAIC PRESS, 1252 Speers Road, Units #1&2, Oakville, Ontario, L6L 5N9, Canada. P.O. Box 1032, Oakville, Ontario, L6J 5E9
In the United States:
      Mosaic Press, 85 River Rock Drive, Suite 202, Buffalo, N.Y., 14207

CONTENTS

INTRODUCTION   KEITH GAREBIAN

PART ONE: THE ACTOR

BLAZING INNOCENCE AND
  PRIVATE WISDOM .... John Connell 3
ONE OF MY BEST FRIENDS .... Timothy Findley 13
CRAFT SLICES .... Keith Garebian 19
THE MAKING OF 'THE LAST
  OF THE TSARS' .... Michael Bawtree 50
FIVE STAR ACTOR .... James Blendick 56
DELIGHT AND TORMENT .... Marti Maraden 60
'THAT LADY'S MINE, YOU
  KNOW' .... Richard Ouzounian 63
EXPECT THE UNEXPECTED .... Nora Polley 67
WILLIAM HUTT AND 'THE
  MERRY WIVES OF WINDSOR' .... Phillip Silver 71
THREE LEARS .... Mervyn Blake 80
A PORTABLE SPHINX .... Maurice Good 83

INSTINCTIVE RESPONSES .... Christopher Newton 93
AWARENESS OF HIS WORTH .... Herbert Whittaker 98
BREWSTER .... Patricia Collins 101
HOT AND SEXY .... Peter Moss 103
VALENTINE TO A CONSUMMATE
    ARTIST .... Richard Monette 106
INSTANCES OF WONDER .... Diana Leblanc 110
PHOTOGRAPHING WILLIAM
    HUTT .... Robert C. Ragsdale 113

PART TWO: THE DIRECTOR

SERIOUS FUN .... Pamela Brook 117
ACTING FOR HUTT .... Mervyn Blake 121
THE OLD FANTASTICAL DUKE
    OF DARK CORNERS .... Barbara Budd 124
MASTER DIRECTOR .... Patricia Hamilton 132

PART THREE: THE MAN

POMP AND CIRCUMSTANCE .... Mervyn Blake 143
TWO MEMORIES .... Barry MacGregor 146
HE AND CLASS GO TOGETHER ... James Blendick 149
STAR BRIGHT .... Keith Garebian 151

SOME RECENT REVIEWS 159
CHRONOLOGY 171
INDEX 185

ACKNOWLEDGEMENTS

I wish to thank the following for their cooperation: Susan Parker, Lisa Brant, Anita Gaffney, and the Stratford Festival Archives; Richard Monette; Nancy Sadek, Parvin Jahanpour, and the Guelph University Archives; Sylvia Shawn; David Cooper; Michael Cooper; Cylla von Tiedemann; Lee Ramsay and the Metropolitan Toronto Reference Library; Leonard Belsher and The Grand Theatre; Robert C. Ragsdale; Peter Hutt; Peter Donat; Patricia Collins; Barry MacGregor; Willliam Webster; Gary Reinecke; Patrick Christopher; and Scott Wentworth.

INTRODUCTION

INTRODUCTION

In William Hutt's acting, Canadian theatre has its greatest example of range, virtuosity, power, style, and vocal eloquence. There is no level of comedy or tragedy that Hutt has not attempted, and there is no question about the volume and lustre of his successes. He has triumphed in Shakespeare, Molière, Ibsen, Chekhov, Shaw, Wilde, Pinero, O'Neill, and Coward. True, he has not had much exposure in works by contemporary Canadian playwrights, but this is simply because there are few leading Canadian roles worthy of his huge talent. Moreover, few Canadian regional theatres have ever invited him to essay Canadian roles. However, whenever a John Murrell or a Timothy Findley has given him the scope to match his genius to theirs, he has fashioned a portrait of unforgettable brilliance. His performances in *John A - Himself!*, *New World*, and *The Stillborn Lover* are the stuff on which theatre legends are made.

But William Hutt's greatness and endurance as a major stage actor obtain chiefly from his body of work at the Stratford Festival in Ontario. He has, of course, appeared in many other theatres across Canada and in England and the United States, but his artistic legacy is chiefly the creations he has fashioned at Stratford where he always bridges the generation gap between past and present. A traditionalist who, like the greatest of Shakespearean actors, can carry a thought through on a single, sustained breath, Hutt also has the gift of picking out a key phrase or word that lies at the core of a speech. His verse-speaking is enormously supple, totally unsentimental, and in its unfusty tones we hear the unclouded summer, sweet autumn, and crisp winter of the Canadian voice. And his acting, which always shows an understanding of the past, is modern in its quest for truth and new meaning. His three attempts at King Lear - made over a twenty-year span - were radically different from one another in tone, texture, and scale, as were his four portraits of James Tyrone, spread over three decades of his career and played in three different theatres on two continents. It did not matter that his Argan for Jean Gascon in 1974 was a huge hit; Hutt tackled the role afresh for Albert Millaire in 1993, risking unfavourable comparisons but triumphing anew. His talent is ripened, not diminished by age.

Only a prophet could have divined from his apprenticeship years that William Hutt was destined to be Canada's leading classical actor who would symbolize his country's stage for the latter-half of the twentieth century. His repertory experience provided him with opportunities to shine in essentially British and American plays, particularly suited to conservative, middle-class tastes. And Stratford in the early and mid-fifties gave him only intermittent splendours, coaxing him to remain dignified in roles that offered him little scope. Yet, the unexampled originality of his voice and the reliable authenticity of his presence transcended labels. And when Michael Langham, Jean Gascon, and Robin Phillips variously encouraged him far beyond the sonority of the classics, Hutt responded with a natural vitality. Not that there weren't occasional extravagances or pompous displays of self-reverential solemnities, but Hutt was the genuine article: his insights into comedy and tragedy, his elegant wit and emotional depths, his gregariousness and reserve, the rapid shifts of mood were all clues to his fascinating qualities as an actor and man.

His acting and private life (often disguised) run parallel in adaptability, for in being the emblem of his country's stage, Hutt has not simply moved with the times but has also remained true to personal standards in a changing world. He has stood centre stage, while the scenery has shifted behind him. Artistic directors have come and gone at Stratford, yet William Hutt remains for all time as a beacon of what it means to have natural style and authority.

This book is a tribute to William Hutt: it takes advantage of the occasion of his seventy-fifth birthday to keep faith with his past, present, and future. There has been only one other book on Hutt - my own biography, a theatre portrait that ended with his achievements till 1988. So, there is ample need for an extension, for catching up with Hutt who could no more desert the theatre than the sun lose its place in the solar system. The pieces in this book are offered, therefore, as forms of further biography, with the implicit realization that the totality of William Hutt, the private man and the public performer, is still too great to be encompassed by individual accounts, however perceptive they might be.

The contributors to this book are primarily concerned with the roles which Hutt has created over forty-six years on stage. They are friends, colleagues, and critics who have all been privileged to have experienced his public world - and in some instances parts of his private world.

Here, then, is a different kind of Life: twenty-six short sketches of a man, an actor, a director, and a friend. I asked each contributor to concentrate on a certain aspect or area of Hutt, so that there would be minimal overlaps. Contributors were given *carte blanche* as to length and style, but where their submissions divided organically into two or three separate themes, I separated the sections to give the book its shape and coherence.

The pieces have been arranged into three broad sections. The first - and necessarily the longest one, given the work of Hutt - includes the technical pieces; the second shows the subject as a director; and the last carries readers further into the anomalous personality of this formidable actor.

Nowhere have I sought to censor or edit opinions. Indeed, I made it eminently clear to prospective contributors that this book was not to be a mere love-fest, and that they should feel free to depict Hutt's personal or professional anomalies and quirks. The only alterations I have made - beyond the inevitable formal ones - are in interviews with Patricia Hamilton, Mervyn Blake, and John Connell, where I took the liberty of condensing, transposing, or synthesizing sections in the interests of unity, coherence, and emphasis. I am grateful, indeed, to all the contributors who offered their time and effort with full compliments to William Hutt, but I am especially happy to have the voice of William

Hutt himself ring clearly in the very first piece of the book. It is a voice that is candid, direct, modest, witty, and revealing, and because it was exercised for a cherished friend in a form of casual conversation, it is unburdened by any need to be performative for critics and fans.

Rather than present the material chronologically, which would have been the logical thing to do, I have arranged pieces with a view to having variety in tone and texture. This prevents the element of predictability from settling like a heavy, dull cloud on readers. Moreover, this also suggests that the book is an album of reminiscences and appraisals, a festive gathering rather than a solemn or altogether nugatory miscellany.

The book concludes with a chronology of William Hutt's career. While this is far from definitive - mainly because of huge gaps in our national archives - it is the most substantial one to date.

PART ONE: THE ACTOR

JOHN CONNELL

Prior to narrating prize-winning documentaries and serving as radio and television spokesman for countless American corporations, John Connell (b. 1923) was a member of resident and touring stock in Canadian and American companies. In fact, he first met William Hutt at the Niagara Falls Summer Theatre, and the two have remained firm friends. Mr. Connell has appeared on Broadway, in film, and on television. He has also written one hundred network TV scripts, with wife Mila, for CBS' The Secret Storm *and* Texaco Star Theatre. *During his tenure on the national board of directors of the New York Screen Actors Guild, he edited its magazine,* Reel, *publishing his interviews with Lillian Gish, Jason Robards, Richard Kiley, Jack Klugman, and Martin Balsam, among others.*

BLAZING INNOCENCE AND PRIVATE WISDOM

(The following excerpts are from informal interviews with William Hutt in Forest Hills, New York, in November, 1989. John and Mila Connell have known William Hutt ever since they all appeared together at the Niagara Falls Summer Theatre in 1950. When invited to contribute to this book, John Connell replied in a letter: "...we had decided the Connell family contribution to your planned paean for our friend's 75th birthday should be your access to the interviews we did with him some years back. I say 'we' because though I asked the questions, the genesis for many of them came out of conversations Mila and I had with him over the years of watching him on stage and being with him socially at his home or ours....He's not only a great actor but a friend we have long worn in the heart's core.")

JC: Bill, you used an expression 'the moment of blazing innocence' for what you tried to find in a role, and I assume that means both comedy and drama.

WH: Well, very often, John, one says these things in idle conversation and out comes a phrase that captures the imagination. There are various phrases I've dug up over the years, like 'acting is the art of being public in private.' 'I've never believed in speaking unless it improved on silence.' Or 'I never believe in moving unless it improves on stillness.' And I remember when I said that line about blazing innocence, it sounded rather good to me. Maybe it was something that came out of my own innocence. But I think probably where it came from is the conviction that all artists, certainly actors, must have somewhere in their make-up a childlike quality, a childlike innocence. The kind of innocence that is willing to accept novelty and enjoy it as children do - which leads to a continually learning process. You never really stop learning. In applying it to a role, I find that very often it is helpful to look for a moment of innocence in whatever role you're playing. For example, the film that we saw, *The Fabulous Baker Boys*, when the Beau Bridges character, Frank, returns after visiting his family and is absolutely astonished [that Jeff Bridges and Michelle Pfeiffer] altered what they played each night. When he found out that they hadn't sung 'Feelings,' he was totally astonished, and it was beguiling, innocent astonishment. He could not believe that after all these years, they wouldn't sing 'Feelings.' As if to change the format was almost criminal! And it struck me at the time, it was the one moment that revealed the totality of this character's innocence and arch conservatism.

JC: There's one in the character of Mammon in *The Alchemist*, isn't there?

WH: Yes, and then the innocence can be expressed in a variety of ways. With Epicure Mammon, [there is] that wonderful scene where he comes in to the two con artists, Abel and Face, who claim that they turn lead into gold. He comes in with a whole basket of lead stuff from his house to give to them and fantasizes on what he's going to do with the money. I remember an incredible speech that builds vision of wealth upon vision of wealth, upon vision of wealth upon vision of wealth, until the man is hyper-ventilating. And the final phrase of the speech is just 'Oh, Jesu,' and I think it must have happened in rehearsal, at one point, when I just simply fainted. Suddenly the image of all this wonderful wealth crossing my mind was just too much for me, so I could do nothing but faint. And, of course, in the production, I'm happy to report, it brought down the house. So, there's the innocent conviction that he's going to get all this, and the audience, of course, knows right from the beginning that you can't turn lead into gold.

I suppose in Lear, for example, his blazing innocence is expressed in his senile conviction that the three daughters are going to play this game of dividing the kingdom up and that each one of them is going to play it genuinely. The audience would perceive, I presume, that he must be incredibly innocent to think this is going to work. The innocence is expressed in the way he treats Cordelia when she refuses. The innocence bursts into a torrent of anger, childish anger. It's like every kid who says, 'If you're not going to play the game my way, I'm going to take my bat and ball and go home.' It's that kind of childish innocence expressed in a violent way.

JC: There's a stark moment in *Macbeth*, isn't there, with Lady Macbeth?

WH: Yes. I think it's all the more understandable when you realize that Shakespeare was a very clever craftsman and he wrote a lot of his plays for his own Acting Company. We know that all the female roles were played by young boys, and I think Shakespeare was astute enough not ever to put into those boys' mouths a feeling or emotion that was beyond them. When it comes to Lady Macbeth, I often wondered about this part originally being played by some twelve or thirteen year old boy. When it comes to the line, 'Who would have thought the old man to have had so much blood in him?' the image in her mind and in that boy's mind is the image of blood, after having dispatched King Duncan in a vicious way with knives. The blood that must have been all over the place, all over the floor, his clothes, her hands, maybe some splattered on the walls, who knows? And she comes down, and the image in the mind is one of blood all over the place. The image is revealed by technically heading for the word 'in' instead of 'blood.' Most Lady Macbeths that I have seen said 'Who would have thought the old man to have had so much *blood* in him.' But we all have blood in us, we know that. But the image is of blood all over the place.

JC: And he's a very old man.

WH: He's a very old man on top of that. But it is the innocence behind it, coupled with the horrid image. 'Who would have thought the old man to have had so much blood *in* him.' It is a technique that Robin Phillips doesn't necessarily believe in, I must say. He doesn't believe that you have to head for one particular word to illuminate the meaning of the speech or sentence or to head for one specific word to illuminate an image - although I noticed in latter years that he has given me the odd note saying 'I think the operative word in this line is such and such.'

JC: Is this a form of shorthand that you two have developed?

WH: Oh, sure, sure, John. You just can't help it. A phrase, for instance, like 'Bill, this is a hairpin line.' It all comes from the playing of Lady Bracknell when at one point in a brief exchange with Algernon she starts off by saying, 'I'm sorry if we're a little late, Algernon, but I was obliged to call on dear Lady Harbury. I haven't seen her since her poor husband's death. I never saw a woman so altered. She looks quite twenty years younger.' And Algernon's line is: 'I understand her hair has turned quite gold from grief.' Then Bracknell says, 'Her hair has certainly changed its colour, but from what cause I, of course, cannot say.' And Robin said, 'While you're saying that line, Bill, see if you can stick a hairpin that's coming loose back in of your head someplace, but concentrate on that while you're saying the line.' So that the line comes out -

JC: Through the action.

WH: Through the action. In other words, you're doing something, concentrating on something and saying something else so that the line comes out loaded with implication rather than just hitting it over the head in a sort of C Major way.

JC: As I recall, you warned Robin early on that there was one particular passage in the play that you wouldn't touch with a ten foot pole until you were well into rehearsal. What was that?

WH: That was the famous handbag line. Because Edith Evans had made such a huge impact with that one line that any time a production of *The Importance of Being Earnest* was mentioned, somebody would come up with 'And do you remember Edith Evans and that wonderful line about the handbag?' And Edith Evans [had] covered approximately eight octaves with two words - 'A *handbag*?' Well, it was extraordinary, absolutely! I mean eight octaves of incredulity! Well, you couldn't top that, and it just hovered in my mind, and that's why I said I certainly am not going to do an imitation of Edith Evans on the line. I don't want to touch that moment at all. Let's just see what happens. And one day at rehearsal it suddenly struck me. When Lady Bracknell asks John Worthing the question about where Mr. Thomas Cardew [found] him, the next line is 'In a handbag.' And her next line is 'In a handbag?' When it came to that moment in rehearsals one day, it suddenly dawned on me as I was looking at Nicholas Pennell, I can't believe this. He's trying to put something over on me, and I'm not such a fool as all that. And all the time I was thinking this, my head kept moving toward my left shoulder, and as my head was moving, the next thought I had was, He did say that, didn't he? I mean, I actually heard it. And by this time, my eyes focussed on the tiny reticule that I had placed on the sofa beside me, and I looked at it and then just turned around to him and said, 'A handbag?' - as if to say, you are actually telling me, standing there with your bare face hanging out, that you were found in a handbag! And that was it, that was it! We had found out how to do this, and when it came to performance, I mean, as soon as Nicholas said the line and I just looked at him, the audience started to laugh and clearly their laugh grew and grew because they had seen the handbag before Bracknell had. They had become aware of it before she had, and they were just waiting for her eyes to light on that handbag. Stage management began to time the laugh, and it was never less than thirty seconds. Half a minute of laughter, just laughter. Until I finally said 'A handbag?' and then they burst into laughter again. It was so understated, underplayed so that all the astonishment was there, but it was in the silences and they knew also what I was thinking. I am absolutely convinced that thought, if it is focussed and precise, has an energy of its own and will communicate itself to an audience. But the thought has to be crystal clear and highly focussed.

JC: There was another key moment that you found later, I believe, that came out of rehearsal also.

WH: It was the sequence in the final act when Lady Bracknell descends upon them in the country and finds that her daughter Gwendolyn is there and, of course, blames everything on John Worthing, whom she considers to be something very akin to a rapist. Her line to John Worthing is: 'Apprised, sir, of my daughter's sudden flight by her trusting maid, whose confidence I purchased by means of a small coin, I followed her at once by luggage train.' I began to think that somebody of Lady Bracknell's social status would find it abhorrent to have to bribe anybody to get information, particularly information about a member of her own family. And there are certain British attitudes that are expressed in the way they pronounce certain words. You know they really don't want to touch those words directly. They want to keep as much distance as they possibly can between themselves and whatever a word or phrase implies. And finally this emerged one day in rehearsal in the way I said the word 'coin.' Also at that point, I was thinking about what it was like on the luggage train. I wore a hat that had a very straight feather piercing through the top, and I thought about what would happen to somebody sitting on the luggage train in Great Britain at the time. It would have been very dirty. So you can see this incredibly erect figure, proud figure, sitting in a luggage train, bouncing back and forth. And I just sort of jiggled my head a bit and, of course, the feather jiggled too. It was funny, but what Robin wanted was to add to the depth of that examination. He wanted Lady Bracknell to point out to John Worthing the agony that she had had to go through on this luggage train to get to him. I just waggled the head as if going through total agony....And that kind of direction that Robin gives has penetrated and permeated and illuminated our relationship over all the years. He's very aware of the fact that actors, and I am one of them, who after performing a play for a certain length of time become conscious of the performance they're giving. They know the effects and they simply head for the effects and so eventually the performance just becomes an indicative performance....And it does happen. You cannot help it if you're playing a show eight times a week. Eventually you have to form some sort of geometric pattern or trampoline below that keeps your performance bouncing, but it does becomes sort of indicative. Fortunately, when I did Lear in 1988, with Robin directing, that was the only performance I had to give that year, so I only gave four performances a week. But even at that, I recognized the fact that halfway through the season, my perform-ance was probably becoming a little self-conscious or conscious of itself. Robin came to my dressing room one night and just gave me a wonderful note. He said, 'Bill, take your subconscious on stage tonight. Leave your conscious mind in the dressing room.' And I knew exactly what he meant. What he meant was, stop thinking about your performance and just do it. Just follow your instincts, because the instincts obviously created, I'm happy to say, quite a remarkable performance in the eyes and ears of the audience and critics when it first opened.

JC: The critic Irving Wardle of the *London Times* wrote: 'On the bare timber platform of Stratford's Third Stage, Robin Phillips directs an Edwardian *King Lear* which reconfirms William Hutt as a giant of the English speaking stage.' That must have been deeply gratifying.

WH: Well, it was, John. It was gratifying not just because of the phrase he used concerning myself, but because it came from a British critic. Very few critics outside of Canada pay that much attention to what's going on in Canada, and the British critic understandably can be quite parochial when he wants to be and sort of imply that nothing good can come from Nazareth. Over the years, Canadian culture has suffered from the proximity to the United States and the emotional attachment to Great Britain. We're constantly sort of Mister-In-Betweens, and suddenly after all the years that I spent in Canada, the fact that a critic of his stature recognizes an actor as being 'a giant of the English speaking stage' means a great deal to me.

JC: Robin Phillips' direction of *Lear* seemed to me to be incredibly simple, clean, spare. Sixteen actors on a virtually bare stage. Did he also do the cutting of the play?

WH: Yes, he did, and the cutting he used was roughly the same he used when Peter Ustinov did it in Stratford under Robin's direction back in 1979 and 1980.

JC: And you played the Fool in that?

WH: Yes. I wanted to do Lear in a small space, deliberately in a small space.

JC: Why?

WH: I think it basically started from the first scene. The first scene - in any performance of Lear that I have given or seen - has always confounded an audience. Why does Lear do this? Why? Well, the obvious answer is there's no reason. He just does it. So, therefore, you have to make it understandable to an audience why he just does it. There's no motivation indicated in Shakespeare's scripts as to why he's doing this, except when Lear says he's going to crawl towards death. But I think it was a party game.

JC: That was the interpretation?

WH: Roughly, roughly that. Robin and I had long discussions about the first scene, and that was the only scene we really discussed before we got into rehearsal. We didn't talk about the heath scene or the storm sequence or the death of Cordelia. We didn't talk about any of that at all. But we were both very concerned that the first scene make absolute sense to an audience....It seemed to me and to Robin that unless we did it very domestically, very simply, in a very accessible way, that it would still bewilder an audience. And his whole concept was we've just had a dinner party and Lear decides to play a little party game...half serious, and half not serious. And he comes on rather irritated that the Lords of France and Burgundy are not present because they've been there for months and they're always late at every meeting that he's ever called. So he comes out already slightly irritated that they're not there, and then he quite casually says, 'Mean time we shall express our darker purpose.' He precedes it by saying you know this and you know that and you know the other thing, now tell me, girls, which of you shall we say does love us most? Now we're going to have a little game here, and the two older girls realize in a way that it is a game. He turns to the third daughter and she refuses to play the game. And the refusal to play the game sends him into a torrent of anger and irritability, and one therefore gets from the whole picture of that first scene that we're dealing with a man who is certainly on the edge of senility.

JC: And that was very clear, indeed.

WH: That makes sense to the audience. It [doesn't] necessarily explain the deep, dark motives underneath, but it makes sense.

JC: Our darker purpose.

WH: Yes, a darker purpose. The rest of the play just simply illuminates the mind of this man. He's a bastard, he really is a stubborn bastard, and Robin said, 'The audience must be and should be unsympathetic to you until you get to "O, reason not the need!" speech.' There's an extraordinary clarity that comes through Lear at that moment when he is trying desperately to explain to his children that it isn't a question of need anymore. Not need. It is because I am who I am. And it's a moment of enormous clarity in the man. And singularly enough, it's a moment of enormous clarity because he himself can't explain it, though he tries. And the very act of attempting to explain makes it eminently clear to the audience. I know it sounds paradoxical, but I think he realizes that he can't explain it to them either because he realizes they're never going to understand or because Shakespeare hasn't given him enough to say. Probably a combination of both.

JC: Well, now, Bill, when you did the role in the David William production in the Seventies, I recall a very different opening scene. In fact, [you had] the courage to [take] that scene at its very height and just go straight downhill instead of moving to the climax at the heath scene, as is normally taken in most of the productions that one sees. Would you think it has to do in part with your own aging and your own deeper insight into the man?

WH: Yes, absolutely, absolutely. You know, the older one gets, John, one's priorities in life become more and more simple. You throw away a lot of baggage that really bugged the hell out of you fifteen years ago, and you begin to realize they simply don't matter anymore.

JC: Years ago, Eric Sevareid, one of our pre-eminent network news commentators in this country, put it this way: 'With public age comes private wisdom.'

WH: That's exactly true. So, the process of just throwing away a lot of things that bothered you years ago makes you begin to realize that they're not worth bothering about. Therefore, your thoughts become much more simple and direct - at least mine do. Much more to the heart of the matter.

TIMOTHY FINDLEY

Timothy Findley (b. 1930) was a company member of Ontario's Stratford Festival in 1953, and later appeared in several European capitals, in New York and Toronto, touring both the United Kingdom and the United States in Thornton Wilder's The Matchmaker, *starring Ruth Gordon. With the encouragement of both Wilder and Ms. Gordon, by 1963 Findley turned to full-time writing, and won the Governor General's Award for his third novel,* The Wars, *which was later filmed by Robin Phillips. Winner of numerous literary awards, including the Trillium, the Canadian Authors Association Award, the Toronto Book Award, and the 'Edgar,' for such diverse works as* Famous Last Words, Stones, *and* The Telling of Lies, *he is as distinguished in non-fiction as he is in fiction. His first book of non-fiction,* Inside Memory: Pages from a Writer's Workbook, *made him the first two-time winner of a CAA Award. He has also written numerous award-winning television and radio series and programmes. His most recent novel is* Headhunter *and his most recent play,* The Stillborn Lover. *A recent winner of the Toronto Arts Award, Findley is an Officer of the Order of Canada.*

ONE OF MY BEST FRIENDS

As I look over the forty-five years since we met, I see a tall figure, graceful but angular in movement - distinctive, too, for its stillness - a feeling of containment that gives a sense of power and energy. I hear a voice: unmatched, inimitable - with its own sense of clarity and cadence. I think of toughness, honesty, courage, caring, insight, imagination - all the characteristics that make a great actor; and not incidentally, the same characteristics that make a great friend. I remember - with love, laughter, gratitude, and wonder - four-and-a-half decades of Bill Hutt.

When we met, he was thirty, I was twenty. He had returned from the battlefields of World War II to finish his education at the University of Toronto. Somewhat older than most of his fellow students - his schooling, like that of many veterans, having been interrupted by the war - Bill Hutt became a member of that miraculous group of Hart House performers who, under the guidance of Robert Gill, went on to enrich the theatrical heritage of this country. Let me name a few of these, because like Hutt's, their collective names are magical: Charmion King, Donald and Murray Davis, Barbara Chilcott, Araby Lockhart, David Gardner, Eric House, and the incomparable Kate Reid. *Jesu! Jesu! The days that we have seen...*

Bill Hutt was already one of the leading actors of the country when our paths first crossed; I was a young student of acting at the Sterndale-Bennett School in Toronto. In the spring of 1950, a call came to the School from the International Players - a professional theatre presenting plays in Toronto during the winter and in Kingston through the summer. They were about to go into rehearsal with a play by Sidney Howard, *The Silver Cord* - a drama about a possessive mother and her two sons. They were looking for a juvenile actor to play the younger son, the one most disastrously tied to his mother. My name was offered - I auditioned and was cast. The director - need you ask? - was William Hutt. Under his guidance - incisive, witty, and sure - the play was a hit. And my career as an actor was given a marvellous beginning.

The following years brought us together in a variety of ways. I guess the truth is, I was in awe of his prowess as an actor - and somewhat amazed at his support and encouragement. As a mentor, Hutt is modest in the extreme and refuses the credit he deserves when it comes to his advocacy of fellow artists.

Ultimately, I was to blossom as a writer and, as a result, it was my good fortune to write more than one role inspired by Hutt's talents. These he has played on both television and the stage. My good fortune has been augmented by his presence.

Bill Hutt has given performances that will live in my memory as long as I live. John A. Macdonald. He brought him to life in the television series *The National Dream*, which Bill Whitehead and I adapted from Pierre Berton's books on the history of the Canadian Pacific Railway. Wickedly funny, John A. was - powerful - almost unbearably moving. Hutt also took Macdonald onto the stage in a play I wrote especially for him: *John A. - Himself.* Oddly enough, Macdonald and Hutt were well matched. By then, Bill had become Artistic Director of the Grand Theatre in London, Ontario - and thus by necessity, had become part politician. John A. Macdonald is depicted in one of Bengough's greatest political cartoons as the consummate actor, playing his starring role in 'Her Majesty's Theatre at Ottawa.' Here, the match took on magic. Given the player-politician character of both men, I structured the play as an evening of Victorian theatre, presented as if Macdonald were, indeed, a great Actor-Manager on the eve of his farewell performance. The first act dealt with his public life - and was presented as Victorian music-hall; Parliament was a troupe of acrobats, for instance, whose human pyramid kept collapsing. The press was represented by a ventriloquist who could make his John A. doll say anything the press required to shoot him down. There were patter songs in the style of Gilbert and Sullivan and a production number about the building of the CPR, featuring Cornelius Van Horne, its great architect, as a magician. The act culminated in an aerial battle between Macdonald and Riel, who was portrayed as 'Louis La Mouche, The Human Fly,' swinging on a trapeze while taking pot-shots at the Prime Minister with a pea-shooter. Macdonald commandeered another trapeze and their acrobatics came to end when he bested Riel. Louis La Mouche was swung into the wings, and when he returned he was swinging in the air at the end of a hangman's rope. Hutt was superb, and might have considered a second career as an *aerial artiste!* But even better was to come.

In the second act - the Victorian melodrama - Macdonald's life began to fall apart; public uproar over the death of Riel, private despair over his crippled daughter and his failing marriage. Both sets of pressures took him straight to the bottle. He still stands, in my mind, trying to justify the death of Riel to one of the Parliamentary pages who has been told to take a stick and get rid of the rats in the Buildings. What comes out is the story of Macdonald's brother, Jamie, who - at the age of six - was beaten to death with a stick by a drunken soldier. As played by Hutt and the young Stephen Ouimette, the scene was unforgettable. And so, for me, was a piece of business later in the act that Bill had tried out in rehearsal one day. The hair on the back of my neck still rises as I remember that first enactment in the rehearsal hall. Lady Agnes Macdonald was played by Jennifer Phipps with the all-out fervour of a great Victorian tragedienne. Macdonald stood, listening, as she pulled out all the stops in denouncing his behaviour. When Jenny was done, Hutt paused, and then reached into his pocket for a handful of coins, which he tossed onto the stage at her feet - the ultimate ironic accolade for a great performance in 19th century theatre. It was electrifying. This remains as one of my prime memories of Hutt, the inventive actor - the writer's best friend.

More recently, I had further evidence of Bill's ability to walk into a writer's mind and to find there whatever it is about a character that has *not* made it all the way to the page. This is what he did in 1993 with the Canadian diplomat, Harry Raymond, in *The Stillborn Lover.* Hutt and Martha Henry brought to Harry and Marian Raymond a profound understanding of human devotion that turned my political play into an

unsuspected love story. This way, too, Hutt and Henry proved yet again
that great actors are the playwright's best friends. I thank them both for
this.

I have memories, too, of the great classical roles Hutt played - Lear,
Prospero, Falstaff, Tartuffe - and his amazing Lady Bracknell. But some
of my favourite theatrical memories cast Bill in roles that are usually not
considered to be central. I remember these - and cherish them - because
in playing them, Bill Hutt made them luminous.

In *Henry IV - Part Two*, for instance, there is Justice Shallow. We meet
him at home on a farm - and the Stratford stage in this production had
been turned into a superb barnyard, complete with living barnyard
animals. Shallow's entrance is heralded by the text - and as we prepared
to see him, we heard, offstage, the sound of a chicken laying an egg. Now,
this was not an everyday chicken or an everyday egg. This was history's
greatest chicken, laying the most beautiful egg in all creation. Oh, my!
At the end of that delirious cackle, there was one of the most unforgettable entrances ever made on the Stratford stage, when that wonder-egg,
itself - supported, as it happens, by the hand of Justice Shallow -
materialized before our eyes. Hutt, as Shallow, had also played the
uproarious chicken and the audience literally cheered. Oddly enough, I
wept - wept at the sheer, unadulterated triumph of the moment, and the
artistry of its creator.

On another occasion, it was not an egg that made an entrance onto the
Stratford stage - it was pure charm. Utter, absolute charm, in the form
of Chekhov's lovely, lost Gaev in *The Cherry Orchard*. Playing Gaev,
Hutt seemed to float a few inches above the floorboards of the stage,
wafting through a dream, in search of the perfect snooker shot. It was a
beautifully accomplished and sustained vision of a man whose society was
doomed by the social changes taking place in Russia. What was so
poignant was the magnitude of the dream that had been lived by a whole
privileged class - until change brought the dream crashing to the ground.
And Hutt's Gaev showed us exactly what it was like to have your feet
forced down to the earth and planted firmly - and tragically - in reality.

William Hutt is a great actor. Period. End of story. Well, not quite, I
guess - because he's also a great friend. For precisely the same qualities
that make him a great actor. He has the insight, the willingness and

imagination to know you just as well as he knows the characters he plays. He has the integrity, the courage, and the honesty to tell you where and when you're wrong - and the generosity to support you whenever you're right.

What else can I say to Bill Hutt but '*Encore!*' And a standing ovation - always and ever. With pleasure - with thanks - and blessings.

Copyright c 1994 Pebble Productions Inc.

KEITH GAREBIAN

Keith Garebian (b. 1943) is the author of three books of literary criticism and six books on the theatre. His biography, William Hutt: A Theatre Portrait, *was a landmark in theatre studies in this country, and he has consolidated his position as a theatre documentarian and critic with books such as* A Well-Bred Muse: Selected Theatre Writings 1978-1988, George Bernard Shaw and Christopher Newton: Explorations of Shavian Theatre, *and detailed histories of the original Broadway productions of* My Fair Lady, Gypsy, *and* West Side Story.

CRAFT SLICES

William Hutt's quality as an actor does not depend on his anonymity as a person. Unlike Sir Alec Guinness, whom he closely observed while the two of them were rehearsing and performing at the inaugural Stratford Festival in 1953, Hutt can have numerous faces on stage, assorted mannerisms, and various tricks of voice and diction without his own personality disappearing completely. From the sere, sombre Robert Brakenbury in *Richard III*, his very first Stratford role, to the tormented James Tyrone in *Long Day's Journey Into Night*, his most recent one, William Hutt's essence as an actor remains constant, and yet it would be radically wrong to characterize his performances as examples of personality acting, because what emerges on stage is not Hutt *per se*, but Hutt's impersonations refracted through his own strong quiddity as a man and actor. Whereas Laurence Olivier, that paragon of actors whom Hutt admired, needed various disguises in order to play his brilliant assortment of roles, Hutt really needs no external disguise. He is quite capable of looking like himself while playing someone else. True, he has resorted to tricks of identity when necessary, wearing tattered and frayed robe and an unkempt beard as Shallow; a specially decayed grandeur of costume and facial appearance for Don Armado; dark make-up, animal hides and

fur for an Eskimo Lear; Edwardian 'drag' costume, wig, and plumed hat
for Lady Bracknell; wig, face powder, beauty mark, rings, bracelets, and
ivory flywhisk for Pandarus; spectacles and full moustache for Gaev;
long, glittering robes for Richard II; heavily sloped eyebrows and a dark,
lank wig for Tartuffe; generous padding and regalia for Sir John Falstaff
in love; or golden wreath and armour for Titus Andronicus. But looking
back at his gallery of parts, I require little or no help from these external
enhancements in order to find the actor's immutable essence. Hutt can
transform his face from within, or - to put it in a different way - he can
find the face of a character within his own face.

On the surface, of course, Hutt's stage personality is a sequence of
anomalies - necessarily so, because, as Cyril Cusack once noted: 'The true
actor, potentially, is Everyman, which is to identify with everybody,
never in mere mimicry, not simply in physical versatility...but in his
capacity to reflect the myriad aspects of the wayward spirit of man.' If
I attempt to piece together a personality from the parts played by Hutt,
I end up with a miscellany of qualities: toughness, cowardice, meekness,
benignity, severity, quietude, passion, vulnerability, sincerity, pretence,
absent-mindedness, masculinity, femininity, intuition, irrationality,
sweet reasonableness. All these qualities are organic expressions of his
true being, but they are not what I mean by his singular essence as an
actor. That essence is the *indivisibility* of his talent and personality. His
impersonations are always stamped with personality, which is not to say
that they are simply a case of shallow or glittering personality acting - like
a conventional stage star's where social qualities such as glamour, charm,
or humour are fully exploited, or like a Method actor's 'realism' where
almost everything is related to the actor's own psychology to the virtual
exclusion of anything else. Hutt's technique can serve any period texture
or style without pampering his own ego or without turning the most
trivial stage businesses into exaggerated rituals. His introspective concentration intensifies his stage presence without being simply a case of an
actor's merely playing himself.

In private, his presence is as compelling as it is on stage, television, or
screen, and he seems able to magnify or diminish its effect at will. If he
wishes to make his presence felt, it is felt; if he wishes to be recognized
when he is in a room, he is recognized. As Bernard Hopkins once
remarked to me: 'Bill can walk into a room with an ascot, and the room
can quiver.' And Hutt's young protegés at Theatre London in the mid-

seventies relish the memory of his arriving at a less-than-elegant drink-ing-hole, where he proceeded to survey the patrons demolishing their cheap tacos and margaritas, before announcing imperiously to the waiters: 'I've got reservations!' On tour with *King Lear* in 1973, he made Soviet bureaucracy sit up and take notice when he reacted to the country's stark, inhospitable austerity by roaring in a Moscow hotel: 'Do I have to get a chit from Brezhnev in order to get a glass of milk in this dining room?'

But this authority in public deportment is hardly what I mean by personality in Hutt. It is merely one quality in the actor whose personality encompasses several rich characteristics of craft. In essence all acting boils down to personality, if by personality we mean a mixture of mind, spirit, and feelings - none of which can be truly separated. In his valuable book, *Mask or Face*, Sir Michael Redgrave advanced the opinion that 'in the end, we judge a player by what he is, even though what he is is the strangest mixture, an extraordinary compound of conflicting impulses.' Hutt has himself commented on the personal aspect to acting. In an interview he gave to Christine Boyko in 1989 for *Preview Magazine*, he said: 'Acting is a very deeply personal experience because you are dealing constantly with yourself in a variety of circumstances. I don't believe that when you get on stage you are a different person. You are the same person in a different set of circumstances.' So, acting is a question of the actor's expanding his 'attitudinal and emotional horizons' as widely and as broadly as he can - but always in relation to the role and the situation in which he finds himself. But, significantly, experience helps coarsen or refine an actor's attributes of personality, and technique helps the actor discover other facets of his personality which are equally interesting and equally true to himself. It should be clear then that, as Harold Clurman once observed, personality in acting could go beyond mere social personality. It could refer to the actor's instrument: 'A person of fluent emotional nature, quick sensory reaction, mobility of inner constitution, a person with an expressive voice, striking mask, natural grace, com-manding figure, imagination, impressionability and temperament, ought to provide the best acting material.'

Indeed! The description fits Hutt in all particulars, though there may be objection to the suggestion of 'grace,' if the word refers only to ease of physical movement. Hutt does not have an athlete's grace - he has always lacked Olivier's magnificent mobility. He sometimes sways as he walks; he is occasionally a shuffler; and in Roman armour he is far removed at times from the motto *Mens sana in corpore sano*. But he is eminently capable of creating beautiful stage pictures when in repose.

It is true that by matinée-idol standards, William Hutt has never been strictly handsome. Although he has aged into an attractive leading or character actor, as a young man or even into his middle years, he would never have provided any competition in physical beauty to John Barrymore, Richard Burton, or Michael Redgrave. When he once sauntered into Robin Phillips' office the first year of Phillips' tenure as Artistic Director at Stratford, the younger man could not help but stare, and as if to drive home the point, Phillips said slowly but deliberately: 'I want you to know that I'm staring at your nose.'

It is possible to make too much of an actor's physical oddities, especially as physical attributes are the work of nature rather than nurture. The perfect height for a stage actor is reckoned to be just under six feet. Nature, however, chooses its own measure, and even God-like apprehension, as James Agate once held, cannot survive dwarfdom or a hare-lip. Agate wrote of an era when 'the critic "went over" an actor as a horse-owner goes over an intended purchase. Is he sound in wind and limb? Is his cast of features noble, his voice agreeable, and his manner imposing? Satisfied with the actor on these essential points the critic then asked him to act, just as the buyer pleased with his animal on the floor asks to see him trot.' The modern actor rarely has to suffer such cynical patronization - unless there is a John Simon in the audience - and greater stock is placed today on mind, temperament, and instinct than on the perfect bodily instrument.

Hutt more than compensates for sway-back movement and an imposing nose. He is a remarkable-looking man, over six feet in height, with a strong physique, warm blue eyes, a commanding profile, an unparalleled voice, and a charisma that can radiate sexuality with ease. Whether still or in movement on stage, he draws attention, but his lure is something deeper and greater than the merely physical. He pulls audiences to him by his own alchemy which presages some complex mystery, even as it makes the disclosure with flamboyance or reticence.

His performance as Harry Raymond in Timothy Findley's *The Stillborn Lover* in 1993 at The Grand Theatre, London, Ontario, directed by Peter Moss, epitomized the core of his acting personality. Refusing to beg for pity, suppressing any urge for pyrotechnical explo-

sions, the actor burrowed quietly into the part. In Findley's text, Harry
is the Canadian ambassador to Moscow who is suddenly recalled to
Ottawa after a young Russian male, his secret lover, is found brutally
murdered in a Moscow hotel room. The order for recall is issued by an
old diplomat friend, favoured to be the next Prime Minister, and at first
this recall to an isolated 'safe house' is marked by politeness and stilted
hospitality by the friend and his elegant, prattling wife, but it degenerates
into a sinister investigation by two RCMP agents, as Harry, his wife (a
victim of Alzheimer's), and their daughter (a sardonic lawyer) are forced
to unravel their pasts. Although Findley is almost perfunctory in his
delineation of many of the subsidiary characters, the play's reality
trembles on the verge of intimate disclosure about the two central figures,
with the dialogue thriving on caustic repartée and disquieting truths
about what lies under Harry Raymond's composure and behind his
wife's mental distractedness. The story progresses through a sequence of
flashbacks which unravel Harry's psychosexual secret. Lies (big and
small, public and private) click like pebbles in a nervous hand, and
questions of politics, loyalty, love, and the inner self are locked into
irrevocable moves and gestures as in the ancient Japanese game of *Go*.
The big question is not why Harry Raymond is betrayed by his old friend,
or whether he will survive the RCMP investigation and his daughter's
high moral attitude. The question is the true nature of his inner self and
the price he must pay for revealing it at last.

The role of Harry Raymond does not have protracted eloquence. Its
growth is in slow increments, with quiet explosions of the heart. But
William Hutt made something special of the part, and in partnership
with Martha Henry, as his wife, sensed intuitively that the play was really
two plays in one ('the play that you hear and the one in between the
lines'). By seizing the tantalizing possibility that what was really important in this play was what was *not* said, he found not only the edge of
breakdown but a doomed love story, quivering with insights into
disguises of the self, of commitments lost, and of love that is stillborn and
powerless in a world of betrayals. As Henry dazzled with an almost
Oriental grace and facility for textures, Hutt acted almost as if in reserve,
quietly watching, suffering inwardly. By not moving unless absolutely
required by the script, by not raising his splendid voice except to his own
devices, he lingered in a private hell, watching his wife disintegrate. And
his psychosexual turmoil never became sensational in a lurid sense;

instead, it trembled with half-completed revelations. Always, always there was a feeling of SOMETHING MORE that could not be uttered, and Hutt turned the incompletions to his own advantage. His sad eyes, drooping shoulders, and pained voice were his own versions of text, just as the half-articulated triangular love story of himself, his wife, and his homosexual lover became a subtext.

This was Hutt as a compendium of technique and personality. This was acting that bore out Ellen Terry's tenet: "To act you must make the thing written your own; you must steal the words, steal the thoughts, and convey the stolen treasure to others with great art." In stealing Findley's words and Harry Raymond's thoughts, Hutt was aborbing the role within his own psyche, bringing his own psychological complexity to bear upon his interpretation. In playing a man with a troubling inner secret and an outer suave composure, Hutt was reflecting his own long-rehearsed but ultimately resolved problem of ambiguity. As a boy, he had felt confused about his relationship with his parents. As a teenager, he had undergone a sexual rite of passage with troubling uncertainty. And well into his mature adulthood, he had had an uneasy bond with his elder brother. So his acting issued from autobiography - without being merely autobiographical. Imagination had acted upon the raw material of text, transforming the baser stuff into something richly layered with truth. And passion - not the loud outcry of a purposeful hero, but the unsteady vulnerability of a wounded heart - was partnered by an actor's intelligence to discover where the ascents and descents of the character occurred. In full control of its ample resources, his acting never seemed brittle or stilted. He could flare when he had to, but for most of the time his fires were banked. He was best when he appeared to be doing nothing, for feeling, held tightly in check, built in pent-up power, and when it did burst through the fissures in his dignity, it escaped at the risk of the character's life. Throughout the performance, Hutt suggested *thought* - even when he had no lines; it was as if his mind was continually engaged, under the unflamboyant temperament, with a delicate assessment of situations. Very much appeared to be happening within his silences: layers of guilt started to peel away, patches of anguish showed, and depths of conflicting emotions were suggested by the actor's full residence in the psychic centre of the role. There was considerable risk to the scale of the performance, for the quietism, though ideal perhaps for film, could have flattened the intimacy of muffled pain. That this didn't happen validated

Hutt's innate authority as an actor - that singular power which combines a generosity on stage with a technique to exploit his slow, investigative, internal moments. As a final finish to a fascinating portrait, Hutt's embrace of simplicity avoided sentimentality. What resulted at the end was a magical enlargement of something tucked away within the actor - perhaps an empathy for a soul in torment - and served a reminder to anyone who needed reminding that Hutt is extraordinarily Chekhovian in revealing the splendour and misery of our life on earth.

It is tempting to play amateur psychiatrist and try to find in William Hutt's background the forces that moulded this man who is superbly gifted, lavishly generous, maddeningly vain, surprisingly humble, courageously truthful, and sometimes diplomatically reticent. He has his anomalies and contradictions, but not all of these are strikingly relevant to an assessment of his qualities as an actor. Those which are have been suggested in my biography, *William Hutt: A Theatre Portrait* (1988), a book which caused more consternation to some of his own family than to Hutt himself. The proof of this lies in our continuing friendship and the fact that we can both chat comfortably on and off the record about everything from Shakespeare to sex, without malignant suspicions of each other's motives.

In all the interviews I conducted about him with colleagues, friends, and strangers, a recurring theme dominated the conversation: What is the *real* William Hutt? So varied are his performances, so widely ranging in tone, that it is natural for his admirers and critics to wonder about the personal core in which his craft is rooted. Hutt himself used to joke in his middle years that he wore an identification bracelet in order to know himself in a crowd: 'If I were on *To Tell the Truth* and they said, "Will the real William Hutt please stand up," I would just sit there.' But did self-mockery conceal a fundamental truth - that of *practical* disguise? Try to portray him, even today, in Freudian terms and there isn't that much to tell plainly and unequivocally: Ego: the modest or arrogant master actor; Super Ego: man of unparalleled distinction with an impeccable sense of service and professional responsibility; Id: a drinker, prankster, gossip, et cetera. What is to be gained by such an exercise, except a peculiarly bureaucratic (and false) tidiness?

The facts of his upbringing are surely not beyond the boundaries of Victorian Canada. The middle child and second son of Caroline Frances Havergal Wood and Edward DeWitt Hutt, he was born in Toronto, 2

May 1920, but was frequently separated from his parents for the first six years of his life while his mother tried to cope with illness and increased family responsibilities. His Aunt Reaveley and Uncle Michael McGarvin of Hamilton served as surrogate parents during this period, and Hutt never quite understood the order of things, though his aunt offered him a warm security. When he did return to his parents, his life settled into a quiet Victorian gentility. His parents were of essentially puritan stock. One of Caroline's brothers had been named after Bishop Mountain, and this same name had been bestowed on William's elder brother. Religion was the iron in the blood, and Sunday Service, Sunday School, and (what Hutt calls) 'numbingly tranquil' Sabbath afternoons were *de rigueur*, as if in counterpoint to customary bursts of wit among adults in the family circle.

Boyhood and adolescence were curdled by his feeling of ambiguity. Insecure about his relationship with his parents - their love for him was undeniable without being explicit - and about his own identity (was he to always follow in his brother's footsteps?), he suffered from a psychological *Angst* that was exacerbated by the outbreak of World War II. Hutt enlisted in 1941 when his conscience bothered him that his friends and brother had joined and he had not. He did not want to kill anyone, so he joined the 7th Light Field Ambulance which was attached, for most of the war, to the 5th Armoured Division which did battle in Italy.

Wishing to make the best of a long, nasty war, he kept a personal diary and grew flowers within a little fence around his tent in a lush valley, where he and a fellow-soldier would sit and sip wine from time to time. He adopted a high moral tone - even in crisis. When one of his men panicked during a particularly bad enemy barrage and just froze while everybody else ran around setting up camp for casualties, Hutt scolded the shellshocked private: 'I understand you're afraid, but if you don't want to do something, don't stand around here. Get the hell out! And that's an order!' But the experience taught him that moments of high tension could be best dramatized on stage by stillness.

Hutt played a valiant part in military operations at Ceprano, for which he was awarded the Military Medal to add to other army ribbons and medals. Quietly proud of these honours, he once cautioned his sister-in-law while they were dancing: 'Don't get too close to me. You're crushing my medals.'

The war years, 1941-1945, crystallized some of his complementary qualities: patriotism, sense of service, quiet courage, composure, and stylishness. His experiences later fed his acting, passing along his dedication to country, his inner strength, quiet conviction, and sense of high style to his stage work. While on fourlough in Europe, he found time to visit theatres in London, where he watched eminent players such as John Gielgud, Laurence Olivier, Sybil Thorndike, and Lillian Braithwaite. Upon his return to Canada, he served an acting apprenticeship at Hart House, Toronto, under Robert Gill's leadership, with roles in plays by Shakespeare, Shaw, Cocteau, and Noel Coward. Dignity and wit marked his best performances - as they also did his summer stock appearances with the Mark Shawn Players, the Niagara Falls Summer Theatre, and Amelia Hall's Canadian Repertory Theatre in Ottawa. The repertoires were wide, the roles abundant and varied, the productions rushed but serviceable. Actors had little time to refine their technique or values of performance, and the most they could hope for was what Peter O'Toole once described as 'a pretty fair shadow of what would be the substance of the part given more time.' Hutt is self-effacingly honest about these years: 'The first thought that comes to my mind is not what [summer stock] did for me, but what it did to the poor bastards who had to watch. So many of us didn't have any formal training. We learned by doing. And there we were standing in front of all these people, probably giving despicable performances because we didn't have that much technique.' It was a double apprenticeship, as it were, for as the actors were learning their craft, so were audiences learning to respond to and discriminate among a variety of American and European plays. 'In retrospect, I really admire the audiences because they just sat there, watching these terrible performances and were very encouraging while we were learning at their expense. Even the directors in those days, aside from people like Bob Gill, were pretty raw. But even then, I don't think we knew what good or bad direction was. We just *took* direction. We didn't even know whether it was right or wrong.' Almost by default, such an apprenticeship was a learning process, although the actors subsequently had to abandon what they had learned in summer stock.

Some of his contemporaries believe that Hutt excelled at comedy in the early years. Charmion King once said: 'No one could touch him in Noel Coward' - a remark that surprises Hutt. 'I remember people saying that to me at the time, and like a fool, I believed them. But looking back, I don't even know what specifically they were talking about. I don't remember feeling terribly secure in either comedy or drama.' So, was the fabled forté in Coward an exaggeration? 'I felt that somehow I understood Noel Coward's humour. Maybe it was because of my experience in the war with the British mind. I don't know. Coward's writing amused me enormously.' His pleasure was compounded when he actually got a chance to audition successfully for Coward in 1960 who was casting *Waiting in the Wings*, and the two men became friends for life.

For all the oft-repeated jokes about Hutt's pompousness and attraction to stardom, the fact is that at the outset of his career, he merely wanted to learn his craft to pay for his toothpaste and not starve in a garret. There were no stars in Bracebridge, except in the heavens, and Amelia Hall in Ottawa refused to recognize star actors, even though she had in her company William Shatner and Christopher Plummer, both of whom would eventually become stage and television luminaries. At Niagara, the stars were imported: Sylvia Sidney, Lillian and Dorothy Gish, Franchot Tone. And when the Stratford Festival was founded under Tyrone Guthrie's inspired leadership, the stellar attractions the first two years were Alec Guinness, Irene Worth, and James Mason, whom Hutt watched and learned from, while harbouring a desire to one day star himself in this theatre.

It took him over a decade to do so - and only after a long succession of supporting roles, which he essayed with flair and authority. In Stratford's earliest years, Hutt distinguished himself whether in full mask and *cothurni* (for the Chorus Leader in *Oedipus Rex*) or in a dandy's costume (as Hortensio in *The Taming of the Shrew*). For the former, he produced a sound that was eerily memorable, like a howl that Frances Hyland associated with 'a great gray wolf on the hillside.' In contrast, for the comic role in Guthrie's antic version of the *Shrew*, he played (in the words of Walter Kerr) with such 'fastidious solemnity' and 'injured gentility' that he became far droller in his quiet eccentricity than had he acted with more volume. Like most of the company, he regarded Guthrie as a father-figure, perhaps even a divinity of sorts. His respect was fostered by the director's enthusiasm for his young Canadians. Over forty years later, Hutt's hero-worship has not diminished: 'I know he took a great deal of joy in my work. He took a great deal of joy in a lot of people's work. I think he gave a lot of us a feeling of confidence. Here we were the only professional theatre, as far as I know, east of Winnipeg, apart from summer stock companies and the the CRT in Ottawa. There may have been activity in the Maritimes that I don't know about, but theatrical history had not started - not really. And then suddenly this giant comes over - the huge giant from England, touted (and quite rightly so) as the greatest director of his age - to direct us innocent Canadians who were learning how to walk across the stage without tripping. I say that facetiously, but Guthrie seemed to applaud everything, seemed to like everything that we did. Liked the exuberance.'

All right, let us allow for some historical inaccuracies from a pedantic point of view and admit to a degree of colonial romanticism - Canadian theatrical history had started before the Stratford adventure - but the fundamental point is solid. Guthrie founded the first truly professional repertory company in Canada worthy of international notice, and he fostered a feeling of familyhood. He was, as Hutt frequently points out, 'the first real father that the professionals had in this country. He started to help all the kids mature and grow.' And what a group of 'kids' that was: Amelia Hall, Robert Christie, Richard Easton, Timothy Findley, Donald Harron, Eric House, William Needles, Douglas Rain, Lloyd Bochner, Frances Hyland, William Shatner, Bruno Gerussi, Donald Davis. The first real set of Canadian actors who formed standards for classical acting for all North America. Guthrie had such palpable pride in his company that he put his actors on display in Edinburgh and New York, even though the productions on those occasions (*Oedipus* in Scotland and *Tamburlaine the Great* on Broadway) did not fare as well as he would have liked. And Hutt received no special mention in the reviews. Guthrie's productions had pace, colour, splendid choreography, and visual effects, but what they sometimes overlooked was that the movement, spectacle, and passion of a play must be created through people and not simply actors as pawns. No matter: the company in general and Hutt in particular appreciated Guthrie's joyous inspiration. Hutt's hero-worship grew even greater when the director invited him to be a part of his Phoenix Theatre season in New York in 1956 for *Mary Stuart* and *The Makropoulos Secret*, even though here again Hutt was not turned into an overnight celebrity. The actor's old Victorian ethic of principled respon-sibility to one's vocation and duty to one's self was well rehearsed. Stardom would have to wait - especially as in the long off-season, Hutt and his cohorts trekked widely across Canada as part of the Canadian Players, a troupe founded by Douglas Campbell. Boldness and a spirit of generous adventure dominated art, as in the first season *Saint Joan* was, in a manner of speaking, carried on snowmobiles and Colonel Reynold's Northland train to literally frozen climes where fur-hooded natives streamed out of woods and bundled together both inside and outside a frosted Quonset hut to watch one of Shaw's most elocutionary plays shrewdly turned for the most part into a mime show.

Hutt's acting experience deepened during Michael Langham's long regime at Stratford. Although Hutt sometimes felt overlooked by Langham in favour of Christopher Plummer and John Colicos, his retrospective attitude is one of gratitude to Langham who, he claims, gave him 'the first faint glow of stardom and the foundation for becoming a major actor on the English-speaking stage.' True, Plummer got to play Hamlet, Macbeth, Henry V, and Cyrano. True, Colicos won plum roles as Lear, Timon, Petruchio, and Caliban. True, Langham imported Paul Scofield for Coriolanus and Frederick Valk for Shylock. But Hutt had a huge variety of roles in Langham's twelve-year reign - from Prospero to Pandarus, from Ford to Jaques, from Khlestakov to Richard II, from Don Adriano de Armado to Shallow, from Sparkish to Gaev - and he was able to leap past a roster of imposingly and boringly dignified parts that he was compelled to endure in the process. Even when he appeared to be miscast - as some thought he was as Enobarbus opposite Plummer's Antony and Zoe Caldwell's Cleopatra - he surprised his critics with an unorthodox interpretation. Whatever his physical awkwardness as a tough-minded Roman soldier, the actor offered an interesting reading for Enobarbus' celebrated 'Age cannot wither her nor custom stale her infinite variety' passage. Hutt crystallized the character's insight into Cleopatra's gamesmanship and theatricality by pausing just before the word 'infinite.' Then he inflected 'infinite' in such a way, as Walter Kerr described, 'as to suggest that he had the whole bit, that he had seen the repertoire of moods and despaired of ever seeing the end of it, that Cleopatra was a con queen who would never run out of fraudulent, if admittedly fetching, little tricks. The line wasn't praise. It was despair.' He taught his critics that the only thing they could expect from him was the unexpected.

His Ford in *The Merry Wives of Windsor* was what one critic called 'an alarmed Puritan of a husband' who was rather sick with jealousy and who shrank from joyous life. This Ford was no caricature, for he was moving precisely because he put all his paranoia into one buck-basket. Hutt's

Polonius, opposite Plummer's mercurial Prince, was no old dolt - the sort of garrulous, prying old bore that Ben Jonson had called senile. Instead, he was a flawed father who was considerably disillusioned with both Laertes and the pattern of life itself, while combining a meddlesome eccentricity with a dangerous connivance. As Jaques, Hutt stood firmly apart from the mess of Peter Wood's *As You Like It*. 'Thank the Lord for William Hutt!' exclaimed Brooks Atkinson. 'He is so much the master of Jaques that the verse poses no challenge to him or to the audience.' A keen sign that the actor was already successfully Canadianizing Shakespeare's verse.

Jaques, Ford, and Polonius, however, were not star parts. Hutt could only star *away* from Stratford - first as James Tyrone (his first of four attempts at the role) at the Bristol Old Vic, while he was attempting to enlarge his experience and reputation in England, and then as an Eskimo - or more correctly, an Inuit - Lear, designed by Herbert Whittaker and directed by David Gardner, and taken on tour in the United States after its opening at the Crest in Toronto. In neither instance, however, was his ambition for stardom rewarded beyond compliments and the occasional photo spread in magazines. The real breakthrough came with Pandarus in Langham's *Troilus and Cressida*, a performance that tapped some secret wellspring of character in himself to feed his interpretation and release him from anxieties about his own psyche and talent. No one who saw his Pandarus in 1963 has ever forgotten it. Part anxious mother-hen, part aging voyeur, he was an affectionate guide to the two young lovers, as well as a dirty old man whose eyes twinkled lasciviously during a parade of husky young Greek soldiers. He exuded androgynous salaciousness, turning the character's bisexuality into an emblem of manipulation. The Pandarus was a case of great acting because it was a driven characterization, out there on stage as a risk - comic, perverse, a lost soul who was incredibly funny while being heartbreakingly real.

After his Jaques in 1959, he had expected great things, especially when Langham whispered only the sweetest praise in his ear: 'That should lead to Richard II pretty soon.' Now the Pandarus revived hopes that the promise would materialize, and Hutt was finally rewarded in 1964 when he got his starring chance as Richard, the self-dramatizing, narcissistic king of shadows and melting splendour. In golden robes, he radiated a sunburst glory. Capitalizing on Richard's blend of feminine and masculine aspects, Hutt was a silky androgyne, ravaged by vanity and homoerotic desire, yet touching in his self-destruction. The actor had become very secure about his acting, realizing finally that he had a matinée idol's quality - a romantic power over an audience. His mother knew at once that her son had turned into a public celebrity as she looked at him with a strange glint in her eye after a performance and said quietly: 'I'm just looking at you and thinking: you belong to the public now.'

The public grew to love him - especially for his comedy and Chekhovian poignancy. No other Canadian actor could match him for his vein of sardonic humour or for his self-defeating assumptions of elegance and refinement. His Khlestakov in Gogol's *The Government Inspector* was ineffably comic - an insignificant young clerk who is mistaken for an important government agent and who finally pumps himself up with grand illusions in his masquerade as a dignitary. As Julius Novick recorded, Hutt's performance was 'the apotheosis of swish' and cleverly appropriate for 'a foolish young provincial who has gone to the big city and would love to be considered a man of fashion. At any rate, a line like "I just [pause] *wither* without sophisticated society" was to Mr. Hutt as honey is to a honeybear, and the actor licked it up with exquisite relish.' But the marvel of his acting was that it satirized the character without ever destroying his innate humanity or mocking his vulnerability.

The Pandarus, Richard II, and Khlestakov revealed his ability to reconcile seemingly opposite qualities of sexuality, but a common thread running through the three was Hutt's sly feminine roguishness. The Pandarus was openly lascivious with effeminate perversity. The toothy smile, the wristy flick of the fly-whisk, the twinkling lust for a husky male body were flamboyantly sexual and a unique amalgam of male power and female seductiveness. The Richard exuded sexuality, but there was an ambiguity in the persona, filled with pain, agony, soaring eloquence, desire, and narcissism. Hutt did not parcel his performance up into a single sexual bias: he allowed the masculine and feminine to interact. As for the Khlestakov, it was silken, ironic, mischievous, vulnerable, tender. Hutt was not afraid to allow all the elements to show, to display *all* aspects of the human personality without shame, modesty, or fear. In all three roles, finery of apparel, occasional frivolity of manner, and feminine tenderness did not obliterate decidedly masculine traits.

In another performance, Hutt showed that he could play an asexual character as well. His Gaev in *The Cherry Orchard* was unforgettable. Certainly he was something of a fool with his impassioned addresses to old bookcases and with imaginary billiard games knocking away inside his head. But he was so delicately bruised by life, so carried away by the mystery of things, that his absent-minded fantasies were deeply touching. At one point he walked carefully right around the stage on the edge of the second step, and resembled an effete figure in this methodical, pointless, time-filling task which revealed his psychological impotence. He also performed a second bit of business, taking out his pocket-watch at one point, looking at it studiously and then saying: 'The sun has...[long pause] set!' Then he looked up at the sky as if to confirm what his watch had first told him.

It was a graphically quiet performance. Often he did little other than remain still, but this stillness was his strength. Many of his colleagues still marvel at his ability to develop a character without much movement. Zoe Caldwell comments: 'I find him best when he's not doing anything at all. I like him when he just stands in his centre. His own centre is remarkable.' To which may be added Louis Turenne's analysis: 'I think Bill is one of those strange people who is plastic in the best sense - a totally malleable character. He goes anywhere he wants to go, with a full emotional and psychological armoury with which to implement the character he chooses to be.' Turenne is shrewd enough to recognize a problem inherent in such malleability: 'If he disappears into the character, it's going to take twenty or thirty years for people to recognize who that actor is. Bill, to me, has always been an actor who transforms his body and voice. Most importantly, he transforms the emotional psychology of himself and becomes the character.'

These comments touch on central questions in Hutt's art and life. They suggest one reason why it took him so long to become a leading star at Stratford. He was too palpably the character-on-stage to be recognized offstage in his non-theatrical person; in other words, he was a character actor rather than a star actor. The comments also suggest the existential problems that an actor faces when he identifies so thoroughly with a role. Gaev was such a lost soul that he was unforgettable both to the audience and to Hutt himself who often wondered what became of the character once he walked off the stage: 'I worry about him.'

Hutt speaks of the link between his acting and private life. 'One of the reasons I was so good at playing Gaev - and I think one of the reasons why I'm very good at playing Chekhov - is that I began to understand in my forties a sense of melancholy in my life, a sense of being alone, a sense of loneliness - not lonesomeness. I began to understand failure - not that I was necessarily failing, but I began to understand human failure. Also, through that period I was beginning to search, not so much for love, but for *how* to love. I was capable of loving certainly, but I wasn't sure I knew how to love.'

Nevertheless, he masked his private failure by a grand façade, even though his panache and authority were a bit misplaced in a country where the public usually recognizes only hockey players or Hollywood stars. In fact, Hutt's insistence on a stylish façade was nothing new to him, for it could be traced back to his first season at the CRT, where Lynn Wilson, the prop manager, recalled Hutt's rounding up all the 'supers,' the assistant stage managers, and looking sternly at them while he remarked: 'If you can't dress well, dress fantastically.' They thought he was putting them on, but he was serious and explained that the public expects actors to look like actors. 'Your gloves don't have to match,' he advised. 'Don't tuck your scarf inside - let it flow.' All this so that they could make a grand entrance at the Connaught Restaurant!

Flair was certainly given play during Jean Gascon's tenure as Stratford's first Canadian artistic director (1970-74), when Hutt not only got star acting parts, but also had an opportunity to direct and serve as artistic goodwill ambassador to Europe when he headed David William's production of *King Lear*. Hutt and Gascon were a mutual admiration society, their relationship being from the very outset one of love. Gascon had a huge heart and an enormous lust for life and theatre. He was utterly a creature of the stage, and his productions throbbed with colour and vitality, even if they sometimes went wildly off track from the text. The Gascon years brought Tartuffe, Sir Epicure Mammon, Volpone, Argan, and Lear to Hutt - four thumpingly comic roles and one tragic part that was not exempt from the ridiculous. Langham had taught Hutt discipline and many things about craft, but perhaps the biggest thing was how to think about technique and a role. Hutt had actually begun to consider content and motive, and not simply the pure mechanics of acting. And to this thought-process were now added the colour, verve, and passion that Gascon inspired by his theatrical zest.

Hutt's Tartuffe and Argan were broad but enormously effective comic performances - the former an example of dark, exploitative hypocrisy, camouflaged by a grave holier-than-thou look and executed with adroit vocal technique and physical mannerisms perfectly in accord with the character's sanctimonious sham. His face a cloying sentimental icon in 'pious' moments, Hutt let his eyebrows hang like heavy quotation marks and his carnal mouth fill with sermons. He was first heard groaning offstage before he appeared with a flagellant and assumed a tone of stentorian piety and self-mortification. His splayfooted movement accentuated his phallic character for he moved as if his genitals hung bulbously. 'Cover your bosom, girl!' he ordered Pat Galloway's Dorine, using the opportunity to thrust a large handkerchief at her décolletage and fondle her breast at the same time. 'Pray heaven, whose infinite goodness preserve your body - and soul!' was delivered to Martha Henry's Elmire, and the heavy breathing, especially at the pause after 'body,' made his true motive palpitatingly carnal. When he uttered 'I long to serve you better,' there was no doubt what was on his mind, as he felt her gown for its sensuous workmanship and grasped her hand in expectation of lascivious fulfillment. His aria to her beauty ended with a gasp of quasi-orgasmic relief, as he moved on his knees toward her. In the full tempo of the seduction scene, he stalked her like a rapist, his tumid lust almost at the bursting point. His 'graveyard growl' (as one critic put it) and preying mantis gait were not in the least mere technical elements, because they issued, like all his other effects, in a fully dimensional human being.

'As funny as a baby's open grave' was once Laurence Olivier's objection to acting Molière. Hutt proved Olivier wrong, and his performance was a signal distinction - far funnier and textured than Gérard Depardieu's many years later, and not as narrow or biliously sour as Brian Bedford's was in John Hirsch's 1984 Stratford production. His second major experience with Molière was Argan in *The Imaginary Invalid*, taken on Australian tour before its Stratford run. Tanya Moiseiwitsch provided the character with a repellently unsanitary green robe, but Hutt won sympathy by revealing Argan's bruised heart while milking all the laughs possible with his wide-eyed baffled innocence. Gascon wanted full comic measure rather than pathos, and directed the production with a flourish of enema jokes, parody, and slapstick. Taste was, of course, brought seriously into question - but only after audiences had recovered from acute spasms of helpless laughter. Clive Barnes and Walter Kerr led the critical raves, with Barnes recognizing that 'On his given night, William Hutt is one of the best classic actors in America,' and with Walter Kerr offering an enthusiastic, extended description of the performance, praising it especially for its 'intense command' of 'silences and other rigidities.' Managing to look like 'a carrot that has already been nibbled on, his florid complexion topped by a nightcap that might have served to swathe a partially wrapped mummy,' Hutt held court in an armchair, summoning servants by bell whenever he could gather sufficient strength. Their tardiness so stunned him that his mouth hung open in disbelief. One of his funniest scenes was when he pretended to be dead, confident that his wife would mourn him. When she poured out her relief instead, he could do little but absorb the shock unflinchingly, as if he were stone cold, yet a stone able to suggest his incredulity.

Sir Epicure Mammon and Volpone showed him off in a Jonsonian vein, both being indulgent performances that wallowed in vulgarity, though there was justification in Volpone's case. David William removed the play from its original period and set it near the end of the nineteenth century. Hutt was not obvious casting in that the Jonsonian manner is very different from the Shakespearean, and in that William dared to emphasize Jonson's preoccupation with anal eroticism with motifs of money and primitive sex. Hutt rose to the challenge with a performance of what one critic called 'jaded depravity,' but public reaction was vociferously against the production.

These two performances and his interpretation of Duke Vincentio in Robin Phillips' brilliant treatment of *Measure for Measure* (1975) resurrected the issue of Hutt as a leading actor. Walter Kerr thought he was 'a meticulous, unfailingly intelligent man with very little romantic magic about him (you feel he would disdain magic and explode romance if either ever came near him).' Hutt had built his reputation in secondary roles, claimed Kerr, 'frequently stealing the scene at hand, but going away without the glory that is reserved for more charismatic types.' As Sir Epicure Mammon, Hutt was not the effete aristocrat of stage tradition, but a clumsy-looking though sound businessman. He stomped across the stage (described Kerr) 'as though both legs had been broken and reset,' and his make-up emphasized a red nose that was not red from drink 'but from the constant practice of sniffing out pleasure.' Mammon's catalogue of unfulfilled desires became 'a musical crescendo,' made especially comic by Hutt's stress of conjunctions rather than nouns. He tasted, said Kerr, 'the connectives, the staggering "ands" (he [said] "*and* diamonds *and* rubies *and* etc."), climbing to each new one as though it were one more unbelievable step toward heaven.' Hutt's Duke Vincentio had 'the benevolent humor of an insane guardian angel.' In both roles, Hutt's

patience with the lines and his cunning with nouns, articles, and
conjunctions were promptly and spectacularly rewarded by audience
laughter. In effect, concluded Kerr, Hutt became 'a new kind of star - a
star who dazzles by being so sane.'

Perhaps Kerr was impressed by Hutt's ability to think in character, to
wed technique to psychology - with the technique sometimes dominat-
ing. But what was that about a lack of romantic magic? Was it possible
that the eminent critic had overlooked the romantic mystery which
enveloped the character on stage? Phillips' production was preoccupied
with repressed sexuality that matched the strictness yet delicacy of texture
in the play's language. The production revealed how the rigidity and
haughtiness of an Apollonian idealism in morality, religion, and politics
could break apart from the turbulent stirrings of a Dionysian force rooted
in the libidinal subconscious. The Duke was subject to this opposition
of forces, for although fond of experimenting on other humans and of
wielding power (even in his disguise as friar), he suffered from his own
psychosexual anomalies. Hutt inhabited the Duke's shadowy corners of
ambiguity and disguise, but his was a self-conscious role-playing as
secretly spying lord of the land. Brian Bedford's icy Angelo and Martha
Henry's passionate Isabella occupied centrestage, where their repressed
sexual desire surfaced with dazzling power, but Hutt, whether in full
regalia of plumed helmet, tassled sword, collar flashes and medals or in
private visitation to Mariana in the 'moated grange,' exuded mystery. He
had an eye for both sexes, and this suggestion of bisexuality deepened the
Duke's mystery.

Two moments crystallized his romantic portrayal. The first was when
he eased a foot upon a stool and handled a champagne glass while visiting
Mariana. This Duke was far more at ease in the situation than he
probably had a right to be. The second moment was his final scene - after
his unmasking and the Jovian dispensation of justice to Lucio, Angelo,
Mariana, and Isabella - which served as a poignant summary of his
character. Circling Isabella for a final plea ('What's mine is yours, and
what is yours is mine'), he revealed a touching tenderness, his rhetorical
symmetry matched by an earnest desire to *share* power. And this power,
which had loosed demons in the body-politic and in man's own body (via
the diseased slums and bordellos, Lucio's concupiscence, and Angelo's
secret lust), was prepared to acknowledge its own sensuality. Hutt's
acting generated questions: Was Isabella to be merely another of the

Duke's bounties - like Mariana, Friar Peter, or any attractive boy that caught his eye? Would he really share power with Isabella once she had satisfied his desire of her? So the performance exuded authority and unfathomable passion, and it was completed only after Hutt (I quote him directly) had examined 'in a very still, smooth, pool-like atmosphere the dark corners of [his] own life.'

Robin Phillips did much more than simply direct some of the greatest productions ever done at Stratford. He Canadianized Shakespeare by letting his actors speak in their own accents and with their own rhythms, set an enviable standard for classical theatre in North America, presented international stars, revitalized even the most experienced and versatile of his company, and refashioned William Hutt as an actor. Despite his ripe young age - he was only in his early thirties - Phillips had already acquired a reputation as a swiftly rising director. At Greenwich and Chichester, he had worked with luminaries such as Sir John Gielgud, David Warner, Irene Worth, Joan Plowright, Jessica Tandy, John Neville, John Clements, Dame Edith Evans, Ian Richardson, and Helen Mirren, so he was far from being green and cold in his judgement of actors. He quickly outstripped all his competition in Canada, despite having to cope with doltish and boorish animosity from Canadian ultra-nationalists. Stratford's company did not impress him much - as he confessed to David Cobb in a 1977 *Maclean's* magazine interview. He found the acting in general to be 'much the same tired old semaphore business' that there was in England and that he had wanted so earnestly to escape.

Phillips was certainly aware of Hutt's considerable and justified reputation as a leading classical actor, but he knew, too, that Hutt had fallen into a trap of convenience, finding it easy and not at all challenging to repeat mastered tricks of acting. In comedy, Hutt's expert timing, mugging, and inflections were hilarious, but the actor would often take the broadest or most vulgar means to ensure the magnification of laughter. In tragedy, Hutt's powerful voice and presence equipped him to reach staggering heights, but in cases (such as Lear) where the greatest tragic feeling required submission to a role and a sinking into the character's psychology, there was a discernible lack of spontaneous openness. While Hutt never begged for sympathy, his technique was a cold barrier between him and his audience. As a technician, he had few equals - perhaps only Christopher Plummer and Douglas Rain, with Plummer being a dazzling virtuoso (sometimes at the expense of the ensemble) and with Rain being exquisitely detailed, though on a smaller scale than Hutt's. As Timothy Findley once remarked to me about Hutt's first two Lears (1961 and 1972): 'Bill's Lears have tended to be gents who were forging their way upward through the tragedy, so that consequently you never quite got the depth of the tragedy. The absolute helplessness had never been there.' Hutt was too much in control. It was not that the depths were missing in him. It was simply that he had not let himself *fall* into them.

Hutt's acting was steered in a new direction by Phillips who encouraged the actor to think anew on stage. Impatient with semaphore acting, Phillips compelled him to rethink his whole idea about acting. Technically, Hutt had always been wonderful - but at a cost to spontaneity and feeling. 'I never felt I had a natural talent,' he once said to Herbert Whittaker. 'That's why I became technical. In 1958, an actress, Arden Kaye, cut me to the quick when she said that I had no warmth in *Private Lives*. It took me a long time to get to know how to feel.' Phillips extended the actor's professional education. Hutt views Phillips' Stratford tenure as a benign stroke of fate: 'He came along at exactly the right time in my career. The right time for me. By that time - though I don't know that I realized this then - I needed somebody who was going to say, "Stop what you're doing and re-think."' In other words, Phillips was urging Hutt not to settle for the same effects or technique that the actor had been used to, but to put greater trust in his own instincts and subconscious.

A wonderful example was had in *Measure for Measure* (1975). During the very first rehearsal of the Mariana scene, Hutt walked onto the stage just as Phillips and his designer, Daphne Dare, were leaving to take their places in the house. The scene had been set, with a wicker chair and a wicker foot-stool before it, and a little table beside these on which was a tiny round silver tray bearing a glass of champagne. A penny dropped for Hutt: the Duke knew more about Mariana than he should have known. 'Absolutely brilliant!' thought Hutt as he sat with one foot resting on the stool. His relaxation and easy familiarity with drink portended a less than innocent relationship with Mariana. Because of the collaboration between designer and director, the moment was extraordinarily revealing. What otherwise might have required four or five rehearsals and much discussion about motivation and hidden urges, was crystallized by a few props and Hutt's impromptu body language.

Another remarkable instance was during the *King Lear* at the Tom Patterson (1988), when Phillips entered Hutt's dressing room before one of the performances and said, 'Take your subconscious on stage tonight.' By that time, he and Hutt had developed a special language or shorthand for their communication, so Phillips' remark, which might have baffled a younger actor or someone unfamiliar with the director's methods, registered lucidly for Hutt: 'What Robin was telling me was "Your performance is becoming too conscious of itself and you have to go back to the subconscious to trust what has been done and not comment on it."'

Phillips had astutely diagnosed an old failing - one that had sometimes marred Hutt's acting in the past - a highly practised technical facility that actually erected a barrier between the actor and the role. Phillips' acute perception and his ability to solve the actor's problem were qualities that Hutt valued highly - so highly that even in retrospect Hutt finds it difficult to describe his artistic relationship with Phillips. 'It's almost mystic in a way - the years of Robin and me...you can sense that I struggle because there is something indefinable. It wasn't that I didn't trust Gascon or Langham or Hirsch or Guthrie. I trusted all of them.' I suggested that, perhaps, it was a different kind of trust. 'Maybe you're right,' he agreed. 'Maybe it was a different kind of trust. Maybe the word is "entrusting" - entrusting Robin with something of me that I hadn't really placed fully in the hands of any other director. And certainly the results were, I am told, quite spectacular.'

Indeed....Feste, the Fool in *King Lear*, Lear himself, Timon of Athens, Lady Bracknell, Bob in *New World*, Uncle Vanya. Hutt redefined himself as an actor, leaving himself open to intuitive insights, fresh layers of interpretation, new trajectories of emotionalism. Hutt's Sir Peter Teazle in *The School for Scandal* (1987) broke the old mould which had held the character ransom to some of the worst stereotypes of Restoration acting practised in the theatre. Played either for blustery foolishness or mannered vulnerability, the role was transformed by Hutt into a pitifully wounded old husband, scarred by his daily verbal duels with his capricious, spendthrift young wife. Deterred in rehearsals by Sheridan's language, which he found to be as difficult as Congreve's, he nevertheless embraced Phillips' vision of the play as a social comedy. His scenes with Sheila McCarthy's delightfully teasing Lady Teazle, grown all apace with extravagant fopperies of town fashion, were filled with rueful, tormented, yet deep love: 'How happy I should be if I could tease her into loving me, though but a little!' Olivier, an earlier, less successful Sir Peter, might possibly have been envious, had he seen this performance. Hutt transcended an old painful ailment - a problem with his back - to project touching despair, melancholy longing for requital, despite being unable to execute all the physical aspects of the comedy as required by the script. The critics generously overlooked this limitation, saying it didn't matter - 'Which means, I hope,' jokes Hutt, 'that the performance was so good, it didn't matter, rather than so bad that nothing mattered.'

In the course of their symbiotic artistic relationship, Phillips taught him to take the pressure off lines - most expressly in *The Importance of Being Earnest*, where Hutt's Lady Bracknell often seemed to be saying one thing while meaning another. The perfect crystallization was in the aristocratic Gorgon's utterance about the dear Duchess of Harbury, 'Her hair has certainly changed its colour, but from what cause I, of course, cannot say.' The sentence seems practical enough in the first-half, but there is a trope in the second where the tone is suggestively wicked. Lady Bracknell's haughty disgust is kept in check simply by the formal dictates of high caste. In short, it is a line fraught with social and moral nuances and, consequently, it could become daunting to a player. However, Phillips helped Hutt relieve the pressure by suggesting that Lady Bracknell preoccupy herself with a minor bit of business - such as the adjustment of a loose hairpin - while delivering the line. The result was a small miracle of apparently subconscious irony, where what was uttered casually enough suddenly acquired a resonance quite beyond the banality of Lady Bracknell's fussing with a hairpin.

Phillips also taught Hutt to control his pyrotechnical power so that the delayed explosions would grow greater in impact after suspenseful restraint. *Timon of Athens* in 1983 at the Grand Theatre, London, gave magnificent proof of this. Phil Silver's set created Edwardian elegance chiefly with mirrors and light. In his burgundy smoking-jacket, Hutt's Timon was the picture of the bounteous man, satiated with commendation. In the first-half, Timon's rhetoric is less than that of his false flatterers who seek to fuel his foolish generosity. But the climactic scene here is the banquet which Phillips designed and choreographed as a version of Da Vinci's *Last Supper*, down to the very geometry of positioned characters. A lurid, slow-motion masque - with tenor of Brent Carver and castrato of Denis Simpson - gave us images of all those things that were enemies to Timon. Then a fire erupted at the end of the long table, a foreshadowing of the smoke and ash of Timon's fury. For his curses, Timon stood rigid with riding crop in hand and produced a funnelling vocal tornado. I could have sworn I heard the theatre shake. The second-half, the sere philosophical one, was anti-climactic, though not without Timon's pain.

Timothy Findley found the production 'breathtaking' and declared as such in a letter to Hutt. Impressed by Phil Silver's décor of glass, he wrote: 'This is Robin's genius - to have set you there, in the midst of all that Edwardian elegance and poise and all those panels of glass - the unbearable grace - the restraint (and what a word that is! The golden leashes at the end of which everyone is let out to walk...) - the sinister quiet and all that glass, the structure in jeopardy - shimmering. And then - the rage, the fury - the heartbreak. I shall never see the like of it again.'

The key words are, indeed, signal ones here: 'the restraint'...'And then - the rage, the fury - the heartbreak.' Phillips could capitalize on controlling Hutt's power because there was real power to control. As Phillips himself remarked to me:'He's the best I know at being able to control his power....When you see him restraining himself, you feel that if he let the lid off, the result would be lethal. It would be a tidal wave. His habit of saying, "Not Yet!" makes you shake.'

Audiences quaked again with Hutt's third Lear (1988). But the triumph might not have occurred had Hutt not essayed the Fool for Phillips in 1979 and reprised it in 1980. As the Fool in an Edwardian setting, he had appeared with iron-gray hair floating wildly around his face. In his creased, green velvet frock-coat, he had looked as archaic as a Victorian etching. His Fool had had a thin, weatherbeaten countenance, and an air of fatalism that showed from his very first entrance that he was bound for suicide, despite his wit. His voice had been as frail as his spirit, and he had moved softly and slowly like one inching closer to the dying of the light.

Was the Fool so good because Hutt had already done Lear twice before? In rehearsal, Hutt had remarked to Phillips: 'You know, Robin, I don't think anybody should play the Fool until he's played Lear first. The Fool knows exactly what is happening.'

And it was also the actor as the Fool who had known what was happening in that production. Closely observing Peter Ustinov's interpretation as Lear as a comically senile patriarch, Hutt had gone immediately for painful wisdom and a tragic bent rather than claptrap levity.

Some audience members thought the play should have been retitled *The Fool.*

When Phillips did the play again in 1988 - at the Third Stage and without the embellishments he had had at the Avon - Hutt found himself once again in Edwardian dress, but this time as a choleric old man tethered by age and folly, yet quite capable of unpredictable spasms of anger during which royal power grew rashly threatening. Here was a Lear who was as quick to draw a sword or butcher Kent and his daughters with words. His rage grew with each cruel insult by malevolent Goneril and Regan, though on the heath it was deep madness rather than towering passion that broke through the storm. At long last, Hutt achieved a Lear who was precipitously vulnerable rather than titanically spectacular, and though the serenity grew occasionally monotonous, levelling some of the peaks in the role, there was a real, battered, frightened, yet exalted human being. The frailer he grew, the more affecting he became. Fatigue, disillusionment, loneliness, scalding sorrow - all the residue of the private life of a shattered king - were revealed in a production that was virtually filmic in style.

Alas, he was never to have that sort of glory again with Phillips, for theatre politics soured things at Stratford, as John Hirsch, the cultural nationalists' favourite, turned the festival into the closest thing to *Kitsch.* Phillips and Hirsch were polar opposites - the former a precise Pointillist or delicate Impressionist, the latter a messy Fauvist or Pop Art cultist - and Hutt aligned himself with Phillips. Hirsch's disappointing seasons were followed by a modest recovery under John Neville. Phillips and Hutt were restored to their stage kingdom with the productions of *The School for Scandal* and *King Lear*, but it seemed that these success became threatening to Neville's status, for Hutt and Phillips were both gradually nudged aside until they disappeared off the main stage. When David William inherited the artistic directorship, Phillips was running the Citadel in Edmonton. Hutt rejected William's invitation to star in *The Grand Inquisitor*, a decision that proved to be the right one artistically, though the wrong one, as far as diplomatic relations were concerned with the gentlemanly William. Instead, Hutt moved to the Shaw Festival where Christopher Newton, as ingenious with Shaw as Phillips is with Shakespeare, gave him three substantial roles as Roebuck Ramsden, General St. Pé, and Sir William Gower. Hutt triumphed in two of these, but his General in Anouilh's *The Waltz of the Toreadors*, rather overwhelmed by the grand set and put off by some weak supporting players, failed to achieve the full phantasmagoric black comedy the part invites. Two seasons passed swiftly, with Hutt enjoying the Shaw and Pinero plays, relishing what he called 'the family atmosphere' at the festival, and appreciating the quality of Newton's work which made human beings out of abstract ideas and ideologies. He also found in Jennifer Phipps an exemplar of subconscious or extraordinarily internal acting.

The nineties heralded the closing of several circles. Hutt had now appeared in both of the nation's leading classical repertory companies. His appearances at Martha Henry's Grand Theatre were significant too - not simply for box office purposes (his Sheridan Whiteside in *The Man Who Came to Dinner* commanded the biggest box-office revenues), but for an important sentimental reason. Martha Henry had supported him in his first Shakespearean leading role at Stratford - his Prospero in 1962 - and Hutt is not one to ever forget a debt of gratitude. Amity is one of his graces. In 1993, he healed some of the rupture with David William by appearing as Argan once again in *The Imaginary Invalid*, proving once again his old mastery at comedy but eliciting pathos at the last, as he shuffled off after his exit line: 'There are no more children anymore. I'm done for. Really.' And in 1994 he closed two other circles by playing the Ghost and First Gravedigger in *Hamlet* and James Tyrone in *Long Day's Journey Into Night* in Richard Monette's inaugural season. *Hamlet* reunited him with Tom McCamus and Stephen Ouimette, two gifted actors he had enlisted for his Young Company at Theatre London. Having opposed Ouimette's playing the melancholy Dane in 1981 on grounds that 'it was too early for [Ouimette] to play Hamlet, and too early for him to fail...[or], indeed, to early for him to succeed,' Hutt was now enthusiastic to be part of Ouimette and McCamus' Stratford success. It was particularly delightful to have McCamus appear, as well, as his sensitive son, Edmund, in the O'Neill. But, perhaps, the most nostalgic circle of all was the one circumscribing Richard Monette. Hutt had been the first one from the Stratford company to have welcomed twenty-year old Monette to the festival in 1965. 'Welcome home, Richard,' he had said, rising to greet the young actor who had walked on stage for his first rehearsal.

The wording was more than gracious. 'Home' summarized what the theatre in general and Stratford in particular mean to William Hutt. 'It's the community of brothers and sisters in this profession that really makes the difference. Family. It really is family,' he has said to me. 'Maybe now I'm talking in a circle to come back to Guthrie who was the first real father that the professionals had in this country. He helped all the kids mature and grow.'

'Grow' - the word should be an echo in every actor's ear, for without the signal element of growth, an actor dwindles into clichés. Those who have seen only Hutt's performances in the fifties and sixties have not seen the fully rounded greatness of his art. Audiences in England and on Broadway who have seen him on one of his exceedingly rare stage-visits have not seen the true range of his craft. They have certainly not seen the arch his extraordinary career has made. Amazingly, William Hutt continues to grow. It is his strength always, the strength of an unparalleled actor ever seeking to enlarge his art and his hold over an audience.

Who thought, for instance, that he would radically refashion the role of James Tyrone, Sr. after having already played it three times earlier in his career and not to the sort of acclaim accorded Fredric March or Laurence Olivier in the same role? I saw the third incarnation (at Stratford in 1980), directed by Phillips, and with Jessica Tandy, Graeme Campbell, and the ultra-sensitive Brent Carver in a star-studded cast. In that production Hutt seemed unduly bland or passive and virtually disappeared at moments when he should have registered more tellingly. But in 1994, his performance as Tyrone was a marvel of re-interpretation. It was the epitome of character acting that owed nothing to memories of Fredric March or Laurence Olivier. Easily capable of rendering a portrait of an old-time star with the yearning of an artist, Hutt emphasized other less obviously spectacular aspects, showing how the miserly father was ruined by commercial success, how the potential artist was damaged by matinée-idol acclaim for melodrama, how his boyhood poverty corrupted his intimate family relationships as husband and father.

Diana Leblanc's marvellous production, so well cast in all roles that you felt there was a real family on stage with real familial interaction, was (as *The New York Times* claimed) a case of 'casting a fearless eye on a sacred text.' Peter Donaldson lent a cynically boyish candour to Jamie's spoiled nature, Tom McCamus captured the consumptive Edmund's poetic sensitivity and fated romanticism, and Martha Burns was also a gem as the saucy maid. The larger jewels were Hutt and Martha Henry. Looking like a pale, ethereal ghost capable of febrile bitterness and rage, Miss

Henry floated in circles or burst into little broken runs, her hands clenched like claws over a white handkerchief (sometimes her emblem of vulnerability). Her tense wrists created a semaphore of manic anguish, her powdered face drew a map of ravishment, and her voice sounded patterns of swooping or darting passion. She was as precise in what she loved or hated as she was mysteriously remote in her drug-induced reveries. She could have been the entire show; that she wasn't was a testament to the quality of the ensemble and the rivetting performance of her counterpart, Hutt.

Without a hint of histrionic excess, he suggested Tyrone's residual vanity. Despite the cheap ascot, creased cotton suit, and dirty, scuffed shoes, his Tyrone had a sense of charming flattery in his Irish lilt that he combined with a careful watchfulness of his wife's abrupt mood-swings and with a deliberate cheer and tender solicitousness. Hutt did not go much for the bluster in the role. Where Ralph Richardson (on film) and Olivier (on stage and on television) had exploited the histrionic scale of some of Tyrone's self-centred monologues, the flamboyance of the drunk scenes, and the showy comedy of the moment when the miserly father screws in *three* light bulbs in an absurd display of sudden extravagance, Hutt did not perform virtuoso set-pieces as show-off moments. Whether down on his knees, searching drunkenly for cards on the floor or suddenly recovering from his apparent helplessness when he discovered that one of his sons had tampered with his whiskey, he used the text to embody the required emotion, rather than artificially inventing an emotion on top of the lines. His was a decidedly internalized performance that illumined the character's loss of faith in himself. With an arm around Mary's waist or with a firm embrace of her trembling body, he was the picture of a man masking his bewildered pain at the darkness of their mutual selves.

Not that he missed his showier opportunities for vocal pyrotechnics - his tirades at Edmund and Jamie had the speed and volume of thunder-claps - but his emphasis was on more revealing matters of the heart. At the end of Scene 2, his crumpled pain at Mary's savage recriminations showed in his slump and in his foggy voice. Here he was the ashen, vulnerable one, needing her to support him off.

O'Neill's play slips back and forth from one plane to another in a painful exposé of tortured beings. Despite the excruciating particularities of its domestic drama, the play has a scale that enlarges realism by a concentration of spiritual torment. And Hutt, with his extraordinary instinct for burrowing into dark depths and then reaching some blazing exaltation of truth, turned his face into a chart of often contradictory emotions. 'I'm not your jailer,' he protested with a defeated look to Mary, turning angry the next instant at her ruses, and then apologetic about his own sharp reaction. He was a man who could not successfully anesthetize himself from self-lacerating guilt. How comic he was in his masks of composure and unexpected generosity! How poignant he was in his almost ghostly exit in Act 2, with a bottle in one hand, as though in further flight from the household torment and his own hollow self! Such moments were unforgettable and balanced against his epiphanies of alcoholic confessionalism. One of the most brilliant moments was his recounting the story of his impoverished boyhood, when he was forced to quit school and work in a factory. This monologue has a poignant force that is compounded by Tyrone's description of how he went on to become an actor and then destroy his talent by a capitulation to a commercially successful but artistically inferior role. Sometimes slurring his words, sometimes using vehement charm, he re-lived various highs and lows of his past - the effect of the actor's art palpably measured by the audience's captive silence. This was romantic, comic, heroic acting, with all the elements commingling in a harrowing portrait of anguish, delicacy, and misshapen love. Its intimacy never compromised its power. Instead of magnifying Tyrone into some sort of demi-god, Hutt allowed the character's weaknesses to show, and yet these disclosures had a paradoxical force. This Tyrone was once clearly a vessel of enormous potential, now cracked by a loss of vocation, a loss of faith in himself and in his family.

In the course of the season's run, he radically altered his key monologue about his early promise as a classical actor. Early in the run, he re-lived the moment of Edwin Booth's high compliment on his acting with almost childish hysterical excitement, but midway through the season, he finished the same recollection with an expression of unbearable shame over his own lost potential. Then, in the silent company of his sons, he sat listening to his wife's final monologue telling of the romance of her vanished youth and happiness, and as night and fog thickened, the scene crystallized into a tableau of tragic resignation. But Hutt broke the frozen moment by a single uncomfortable shifting of his body, indicating by this movement the character's haunting guilt. The slight movement improved on the stillness, clarifying the moment rather than distracting from it. Grief over a hauntingly wasted life was partnered by a sense of falsehood within himself and by the shocking burden of his deeply disturbed wife. Long practised in the art of pretence, Tyrone could no longer pretend that he could transcend his burdens. Hutt's technique was once more fused with his acting personality, and his hold over his audience was mesmerizing. By expressing the deep crises of the role through his own spirit, Hutt seemed as true and as moving a James Tyrone as has ever been experienced.

Whatever the future bodes for him, Hutt has shown convincingly that his dignified reputation has nothing to do with being retired from the often tortuous process of distilled art. He continues to take risks in big roles because he believes that a rehearsal of facile acting tricks simply leads to what he calls 'very shallow waters.' And as he insists, 'I'd rather be a big failure than a shallow success.' As ever, the best of his work has remained rooted in real life and in a personality of such easeful authority that the perfect discipline of his stage personae is at one with the essence of his own emotional experience. This actor is unique and unforgettable.

MICHAEL BAWTREE

An Australian by birth, Michael Bawtree (b. 1937) immigrated to Canada in 1962 after graduating from Oxford University. He became the first resident dramaturge at the Stratford Festival in 1964, before stints at Simon Fraser University (to establish its drama program) and at the National Arts Centre. Upon his return to Stratford, he went on to become Literary Manager, the first director of the Third Stage, and assistant to the artistic director. In addition to writing The Last of the Tsars, *which was performed at Stratford in 1966, Mr. Bawtree directed several productions, including Oliver Goldsmith's* She Stoops To Conquer, *Murray Schafer's opera* Patria II, *and Gabriel Charpentier's* Orpheus. *In 1975, he helped found Comus Music Theatre, and some of his subsequent distinctions include being head of the Banff Centre School of Fine Art's summer musical-theatre program and the author of* New Singing Theatre.

THE MAKING OF *THE LAST OF THE TSARS*

Bill Hutt was one of many who had a challenging year in 1966 with 'the Russian play.' Stratford had first commissioned William Kinsolving to write a play about the Russian Revolution. Kinsolving's *Nicholas Romanov* rehearsed in Stratford, and then was moved to Winnipeg in March to open at the Manitoba Theatre Centre. Bill was cast in the title role, and brought his unique kingliness to the part: a Tsar is born. Unfortunately, Michael Langham, who had directed the piece, was deeply dissatisfied with it, and I was flown in from Vancouver to serve as a kind of play doctor. Stuffed with advice, poor William Kinsolving went away to re-write his piece, and a few weeks later I got an anguished call from Michael to say that the new version had arrived, and that he was even more dissatisfied than before. He asked me to take over the re-writes. I said that I felt the basic concept was a problem, and that really a new play was needed. Michael invited me to write that play. I said he was crazy - there were only six weeks before the first rehearsal. He said: 'Look, you have one of the finest companies in North America, with one of the greatest of all designers (Leslie Hurry), a wonderful composer (Lou Applebaum), and a reasonably good director. Even half the tickets have been sold. What playwright could refuse such an opportunity?'

I capitulated, and *The Last of the Tsars* was conceived.

Michael did not immediately tell the Festival's Board of his decision to drop the Kinsolving play, because he felt they might not be able to cope. He thus took entirely on himself the responsibility for inviting me to write a replacement play. When Floyd Chalmers, then Board president, discovered in late May what was going on, he was extremely angry, as Michael had predicted he would be. But, as Michael had also calculated, it was by then too late to do anything about it. With the company, however, Michael had to be straightforward from the beginning, and he was facing a potentially difficult situation. Actors were contracted to play characters in a play which had been discarded, and then had to wait to find out what the new play would offer them, either in the same character or in another. Only faith in Michael brought them through - that, and Bill's leadership of the company during those strange weeks. Bill himself had in fact to suffer the biggest sea-change.

It had been clear to me that what the chaotic historical material urgently needed was a dramatic viewpoint, and I therefore chose the Tsar's maverick brother Grand Duke Michael to serve as narrator for the play, both outside and within the story of Tsarist Russia's decline and fall. Grand Duke Michael thus became the starring role of the new play, and Michael Langham had the job of approaching Bill and asking him to switch parts. The loss of royal seniority was perhaps compensated for by the fact that Bill was still playing the title role: when Tsar Nicholas abdicated in 1917, he had handed over power to this same brother Michael, who for 48 hours reigned as the Tsar - 'the last of the Tsars.'

Frances Hyland, incidentally, who had been playing the Tsarina in *Nicholas Romanov*, felt that her new incarnation in my play was less sympathetic than before, and decided she would prefer not to continue in the part - which in the end was performed with wonderful strength and pathos by Amelia Hall. Frances gallantly agreed to stay on in the company, and became first the Tsarina's confidante, Anna, and later a powerful peasant woman in the crowd. These dynastic upheavals were completed when at my suggestion Stratford approached Joel Kenyon to play the Tsar. It was the first of many Stratford seasons for Joel.

Michael's shouldering of the entire responsibility for the change of play was courageous, but of course depended entirely on his faith in me, and in my being able to come up with a new piece double-quick. This was daunting: I had never completed a full-length play before.

I was to write the play at Michael's house on Trow Avenue, Stratford. But first I had to return to Vancouver for two weeks to disentangle myself from other engagements. I set to work at once, undertaking an enormous amount of research and even sketching a draft of the first twenty pages. Then, while stepping into the car one fine spring morning to drive to the airport and fly to Stratford, I left my briefcase on the car-roof. I only discovered the loss on the plane.

Michael was a wee bit alarmed next morning at breakfast when I broke the news. But in fact I was able to re-create the pages within 24 hours; and when the postman found my case in the buses a few days later and mailed it on, there were few changes to be made.

I worked in Michael's dining-room (Helen, his wife, had not yet come out from England that year), on an old Remington brought over from the theatre. Michael went off to work every day, and would return at about five. 'How's it going?' he would ask, breezily. 'Four and a half pages today,' I would reply. 'Great. Have a drink,' he would say - or, if I wanted to keep going for a while, he would drop over and see John Hayes next door.

When the first draft of the first act was completed - and not before - I gave it to him to read. 'Fine,' he said. 'I have a few ideas, but keep going.' There were now just under three weeks to the first day of rehearsal, but Michael's perpetual calm was astonishing, and gave me enormous confidence. Perhaps the play really would be finished, and on time.

Then, halfway through the second act, with countless strands of action simultaneously in the play, I got stuck. For a whole day I couldn't produce a word. 'How's it going?' asked Michael when he returned from the theatre. 'Nothing,' I said miserably: 'I just can't get anything to work.' Michael didn't miss a beat. 'Don't worry,' he said, smiling and relaxed as ever. 'These things happen. You'll be fine tomorrow.' And he would leave me agonizing for another hour or so before dinner.

The next day the same thing happened, and once again Michael was calm and confident, getting out of my way for another tortured hour. I tried everything - walks by the river, hot baths, phone-calls to friends, Agatha Christie, double scotches. Nothing helped: for a third day my page was a blank, and only Michael's still imperturbale faith kept me from taking the first train out. But then that night, some time between sleep and wake, an amazing thing happened. I GOT it: three pages of text suddenly sprang complete into my mind, weaving the play's strands together and breaking the deadlock. I rose early, and had the pages written out by breakfast.

Within another week the second act was complete, leaving about five days to work on a second draft. Michael's advice and suggestions were invaluable: I was still much too close to it all to know what I had written. During one or two of those final evenings I would walk over to the Avon and stand there on the stage alone in the darkened theatre, reading my script aloud to test its rhythms. On the first day of rehearsals the cast had the first act in their hands. By the afternoon of the next day they were able to read the play through to the end.

William Kinsolving's lawyers naturally demanded to see my text - concerned that I might have lifted sections from the previous work. But it really was a new work, a fact they soon graciously acknowledged. Kinsolving was disappointed and hurt by the turn of events, and I felt badly about this. I imagine he assumed I had used my position as play doctor to pronounce the patient dead and then to muscle in on replacing him. But I have to say that this was not the case: it was Michael's insistence, based on his conviction that *Nicholas Romanov* could never work, which led to such a drastic change of plan.

The fact that I had been dramaturge of the Festival two years earlier, and so knew all the members of the company extremely well, meant that I had been able to tailor the work to the cast, and apart from Frannie's decision to switch roles, I heard of no serious problems, although there was a whole new play to create and new parts to grapple with and memorize. It was gratifying that fine actors like Amelia Hall, Powys Thomas, and Tony van Bridge liked their dialogue and found it good to speak. (Tony did insist on changing the word 'fuck' to 'rape,' but then this was 1966!).

Bill soon understood that his role as the narrator Grand Duke Michael required him to be a charming host, never losing the grace and ease of royalty, never at a loss. He played the part with consummate urbanity, and had much to do with the production's considerable success when it opened on July 12th.

It was over twenty years later that I was sharing the memory of those days with John Hayes, and telling him how Michael's confidence in me had been instrumental in my being able to finish the job: how wonderfully calm he had been, even when I was stuck with writer's block. 'Calm?' said John. 'My God, you should have seen him bursting in here every evening, pale as a sheet, and stammering, "For God's sake, Michael hasn't written anything for a whole day. He'll never make it. What am I going to do? What am I going to tell the Board? Please, John, a drink - quick. Make it a big one.'"

So there we are. They always say directors should know how to act.

JAMES BLENDICK

A prominent Canadian stage actor, James Blendick (b. 1941) is equally at home on a stage or in front of a camera. His theatre roles include Claudius, Falstaff, Big Daddy, Lopakhin, Sir Toby Belch, and Simon Eyre at Stratford; Pizzaro, Duke Vincentio, and Poche/Victor Emmanuel at the Manitoba Theatre Centre; and Cyrano, Kent, John Proctor, and Bottom at the Guthrie Theatre in Minneapolis. He has also appeared at the Lincoln Centre and on Broadway. His numerous Canadian television credits include leads in Lulu Street, Street Legal, Macbeth, A Midsummer Night's Dream, The Three Musketeers, *and* For The Record, *while his American television credits include appearances in* Police Story, The Invisible Man, Kojak, Bionic Woman, Incident in a Small Town, *and* Underground to Freedom. *In film, he has acted with Cliff Robertson, Don Johnson, and Rebecca de Mornay. Mr. Blendick is the winner of two Canada Council Awards and a Tyrone Guthrie Award.*

FIVE STAR ACTOR

To start with - and I know this has been said many times before, but I'll say it again and keep on saying it - William Hutt is one of the English-speaking world's Great Stage Actors. The flexibility of his mind to invent is extraordinary. His presence, vocal ability, childlike vulnerability, sensitivity, panache, comedic sense and timing, gift of listening, and sense of interpretation have proven him to be perfection in many instances.

I first met Bill when Michael Langham asked me to join the Stratford company in 1967. That year had one of the most star-studded casts - Zoe Caldwell, Alan Bates, Bill Hutt, and Chris Plummer. I had just graduated from the National Theatre School and, needless to say, I was very excited and at the same time extremely terrified.

But Bill Hutt was very kind and helpful to us who were young, aspiring actors. He always seemed to have time to listen to us and to be encouraging. He was always available to those individuals who were honestly willing to learn what the business of acting is all about.

Bill has said that he does not suffer fools gladly. He is quick to spot a fraud and his motives, just as he is quick to spot the genuine article.

It was very difficult yet exhilarating as a young actor to come on stage and be challenged by Bill's great presence - especially in *The Government Inspector* where he was an absolutely outstanding Khlestakov. But I knew that he was always aware of the state and level of maturity of actors he was dealing with in a scene, and that he would always give them their moment 'in the sun.' This generosity is not so true of many other actors I have worked with in my twenty-seven years in the business.

Bill's creative powers as an actor started to fall into place at this time. Everything seemed to work in his acting. I know Michael Langham always did believe in Bill's talent. He as well as others knew that Bill would not be denied the great parts of the theatre.

Bill has always seemed to me to have a great gift of patience - especially about his career. I remember him telling a story about when he was a younger actor with the Stratford company. He was in his dressing room, readying for a show, and while staring into the mirror, he said prophetically, 'One day I will be a leading actor with this company and play the great roles of Shakespeare, Chekhov, Jonson, and so on.'

This story shows how his patient, careful determination, faith in his own ability, and willingness to learn his craft on all levels have made him one of the important and great actors of our time.

Bill has a wonderful sense of what the creative temperature should be when rehearsing a play. When there have been heated disagreements between actor and director or when actors or directors choose to be hostile, arrogant, all-knowing, and rude, Bill grows very quiet and will eventually retire to his dressing room, not without also suggesting a coffee-break with the hope of returning to an atmosphere of civility and relaxed ease. Bill is very aware of the importance of the creative climate, and he is not willing to compromise that.

As a fellow actor, of course, it is always exciting to anticipate what he will do with a part. You know when you go to the theatre to see him perform that something unusual is about to happen. It becomes an event as well as an education to those of us in the business who are aspiring to be better than we are. He has become part of history with the Stratford Festival, and he's also one of the few actors I know who has had and continues to have a consistent love affair with his audiences. He likes nothing better than to please them.

It has been said that Mr. Hutt is a Very Grand Person. That I think is true. But why not? He's proud of his accomplishments, he loves his life, his family, his friends, his theatre family, Theatre itself. I would say that that is a good reason to be proud. Why bury himself in false humility?

He is simply secure about being Bill Hutt. He's committed to and proud of his profession, as well as being very protective of the theatre community which has not always been well looked upon. He believes this community to be a vital creative and contributing force to the culture of this country - a country he loves, a country he has literally fought for. And the wonderful thing is that Bill stayed in this country of ours and built an international reputation.

Unlike so many other Canadian actors, including myself, who have sought fame and fortune down south and elsewhere, he did it here in Canada. Apart from a three-year sojourn in England, some U.S. and European tours, and a brief period of time in New York with two or three productions - including *Tiny Alice* - he has not left Canada for long. Yet he's well-known and respected abroad. I worked for a period of sixteen years in the U.S., from New York and Los Angeles to Washington and San Diego, and whenever American actors learned I was from Canada, they would ask without hesitation, 'Do you know William Hutt?' It's extraordinary when you think of it.

We who have had the opportunity to be a part of his journey as a colleague are truly, truly blessed.

MARTI MARADEN

After substantial credits as an actress, most notably at the Stratford and Shaw Festivals where she played leads such as Miranda, Ophelia, Juliet, Portia, Roxanne, and Cleopatra, Marti Maraden (b. 1945) turned to directing and has successfully staged everything from Michel Tremblay and Shaw to O'Neill, Coward, Corneille, and Shakespeare at the Grand Theatre, Tarragon Theatre, the Canadian Stage Company, and the two festival repertories where she had earned many of her earlier acting notices. She served as Director of the Young Company at Stratford (1992-93).

DELIGHT AND TORMENT

William Hutt as Aunt Agatha (Lady Bracknell to most) was to me a delight and a torment. A delight because I'd feared that casting a man in the role might result in pantomime dame camp, but I soon discovered that Bill would play her with discretion and as a *lady* to the very top of the feather (some six feet, seven inches off the floor) on his Queen Mary hat. A delight, too, because he contributed so much to a fond and happy atmosphere within the cast.

Now, as to torment: Bill soon discovered that I was a hopeless giggler (reading stories of Olivier's problems with this affliction has always been a great comfort to me). He realized that his very peculiar Lady Bracknell rendition of words like 'coin' and 'point' - which became something like 'coern' and 'poernt' - would send me into paroxysms of poorly-concealed laughter.

Eventually I more or less inured myself to these peculiarities.

But then one day Bill uttered the line: 'I need hardly tell you that in families of high position, strange coincidences are not supposed to occur,' and managed to skew the 'oin' in 'coincidences' in a similar fashion. I was lost.

As a director today, I will say frankly that I would be disinclined to cast a man as Lady Bracknell as there are so very many fine women who ought to have a chance to play this splendid Gorgon. Nevertheless, I will always remember *and* with great pleasure the delight and torment of Bill's towering lady.

RICHARD OUZOUNIAN

In his twenty-three years in professional theatre, Richard Ouzounian (b. 1950) has written, directed, or acted in over 200 shows. He has been the Artistic Director of Young People's Theatre, Festival Lennoxville, the Manitoba Theatre Centre, CentreStage Company, and the Neptune Theatre. He spent four years as an Associate Director of the Stratford Festival, and served as Assistant to Hal Prince on the Canadian production of The Phantom of the Opera. *For the last five seasons, he has hosted* Say It With Music, *the popular musical theatre show on the CBC Stereo Network, and is also the Theatre Critic for CBC's* Later The Same Day *in Toronto.*

'THAT LADY'S MINE, YOU KNOW'

When I heard that Robin Phillips had cast William Hutt as Lady Bracknell, I was dubious. It sounded like a gimmick at the best, and at the worst, it smacked of exploitation of the lowest order.

Consequently, I flew out from Vancouver to see the production with so many misgivings that I nearly had to pay for excess baggage.

I should have known better. Phillips is an artist, and Hutt has never been anybody's fool.

What was the performance like? It was dry, but not dry in the manner of pressed flowers or dusty libraries. It was dry the way a good Spanish sherry is dry, with warmth and bite and resonance lurking behind the surface aridity.

Hutt's Lady Bracknell had seen the world, and not approved of very much of it. The eyes were heavily hooded, like a dyspeptic cobra's, and when they turned their attention to the unfortunate John Worthing, one feared for his life.

'To lose one parent, Mr. Worthing, may be regarded as a misfortune...' The head was tilted back ever so slightly, the poison sacs were ready. '...to lose both...'...a short but deadly pause...'looks like carelessness.'

And with a flip of the head, the venom went spewing, and the poor young man was left reeling.

How did Hutt deliver the famous line 'A handbag?'? Well, I seem to remember a case of calculated underkill. The voice dropped low at the sheer horror of it all, as though forced to describe an unspeakable act. There was certainly no cheap grovelling for a laugh.

That was the astonishing thing. By not asking for laughter, Hutt's Lady Bracknell gathered bushels of it. But this performance was more than funny. It was also sensible. The good solid stuff that empires were built on.

It seems strange to compare William Hutt to Gene Kelly, but that's what went through my mind. Not the Kelly of the flashing feet, but the Kelly of *Singing in the Rain*, whose Don Lockwood loved to assure us that his personal motto was 'Dignity, always Dignity.'

A performance I remembered vividly...especially on a night in Spring some seven years later.

At that point, I was Artistic Director of the Manitoba Theatre Centre, and had just opened a production of *The Importance of Being Earnest* featuring a lovely performance by Maggie Askey as Lady Bracknell.

Unfortunately, the morning after the opening, Ms. Askey fractured her hip stepping out of her bath, and we were without an understudy. The three weekend performances were sold out, however, and the show had to go on.

And so, remembering Hutt's Lady Bracknell, I stepped into the breach.

While I tried my best to remember his performance, Mr. Hutt and I are decidedly different performers. He was raised in the classical theatre, I in the world of musical comedy. Consequently, my efforts at dignity got no further than a rough approximation of Angela Lansbury.

My emergency performance, however, was widely publicized, and word of it even reached Mr. Hutt. Because, when we next met, a year later, he fixed me with that basilisk gaze of his, and said, 'I understand you've been playing my part.'

One took for granted that he wasn't referring to King Lear.

I allowed that I had, but only for three performances.

'I heard you were rather good,' he offered, with his typical generosity.

'Oh, no,' I began, and then went on to insist on how I was just the Bus and Truck imitation of his pristine original.

He seemed delighted by my comments, because he smiled and said, 'Good. Just don't play it again.' And at this point, he looked over his shoulder, before continuing with a wicked grin.

'Because that Lady's mine, you know, *all* mine.'

I couldn't agree more.

NORA POLLEY

Born in Stratford (1947), Nora Polley came to her vocation as Production Stage Manager with impeccable credentials. Her father, Victor, had begun working at the Stratford Festival in 1954, and had risen to the position of Administrative Director. Ms. Polley was appointed Stage Manager in 1969, and subsequently went on to increase her distinctions, becoming Associate Director in 1992 and 1993 and Manager for the John Sullivan Hayes Programme for Theatre Training. Theatres across Canada have welcomed her expertise.

EXPECT THE UNEXPECTED

My father began working at the Stratford Festival in 1954, so I have known William Hutt most of my life. Over the years, my mother referred to him as THE VOICE when he called our home to speak to Dad. I'm sure she would have purchased any product, had Bill done the commercial voice-over.

I first worked with Bill in 1969. I was an apprentice in Stage Management at the Festival and Bill was a star - Sir Epicure Mammon in *The Alchemist*, the Duke in *Measure For Measure*, and Tartuffe in *Tartuffe*. I began to understand what my mother meant by THE VOICE - those seductive, resonant tones that mesmerize an audience.

When I stage managed *King Lear* four years later, he had the title role. It was that summer that I learned to expect the unexpected from Bill.

All of us of a certain age know where we were when Paul Henderson scored the winning goal in the final Canada-Soviet hockey game in 1972. I was in the Festival Stage Management booth calling the cues for *King Lear*. The student audience was rather restless and many were listening to the game on surreptitious portable radios. The cast was fighting a losing battle to gain their undivided attention. At the end of the storm scene on the heath, Bill was exiting down the right tunnel.

He stopped, scanned a sea of distracted pubescent theatre-goers, then bellowed, 'Henderson scored. Canada won 6 to 5!' The audience went through the roof: Bill left the stage amid a din unlike anything I had experienced since the Beatles' Labour Day concert in 1964.

After what seemed like forever, I cued on Barry MacGregor and Powys Thomas who opened the next scene. After the unprecedented uproar, an equally awesome hush fell over the theatre, and the students listened attentively until the end of the play.

I have always been of two minds about Bill's interjection - but he did win the audience over to our side for the rest of the show.

Later that same season, Bill broke the fourth wall - the invisible barrier between stage performer and audience - yet again. Throughout a *Lear* student matinée, he had been taunted by several rather drunken teenagers seated in the balcony. When Bill made his final entrance carrying the dead Cordelia in his arms, they mocked his plaintive 'Howl, howl, howl.' Bill announced that if the hecklers were not silent, he would stop the show. Having broken his own concentration so badly, Bill found he could not continue. He set a startled Elizabeth Shepherd on her feet and left the stage. The rest of the company followed, except for Pat Galloway and Carole Shelley who were lying dead under a tarpaulin on the right door landing. My assistant made an unscheduled entrance to help the two actors offstage - and *Lear* was over, the King, uniquely perhaps, still very much alive and kicking.

Over the years, I have worked with Bill on many wonderful projects, including Robin Phillips' 1983-84 Repertory Season at the Grand Theatre in London, which featured Bill and John Neville in drag as the spinster sisters in *Arsenic and Old Lace*. I also stage managed *Darrow*, a one-man show about the famous American lawyer, produced by The Playhouse in Vancouver.

Successful one-person shows are true feats of concentration and theatre-craft; Bill was anxious to find some sort of communication between us that could be used should he ever dry during a performance.

Darrow's wife was named Ruby; she worked as his manager, accompanying Darrow on all his lecture tours. It was determined that if Bill ever needed my help with a line, he would say, 'Where am I, Ruby?' and I would prompt.

This was necessary only once during the run of *Darrow*, but I always felt especially close to Bill during those performances. After all, I was his 'Ruby.'

Happy birthday, Bill.

PHILLIP SILVER

A much honoured set, costume, and lighting designer, who has won three Dora Mavor Moore Awards, a Sterling Award, the Alberta Achievement Award, the City of Edmonton Performing Arts Award, and the Queen's Silver Jubilee Medal, Phillip Silver (b. 1943) has worked at major theatres across this country - including the Stratford Festival, the Shaw Festival, the Citadel Theatre, Neptune Theatre, Canadian Stage Company, the Edmonton Opera, Vancouver Opera, L'Opéra Québec, and the Alberta Ballet Company. While he was Resident Designer at the Citadel (1967-78), he served as consultant on theatre architecture and design for the Shoctor and Rice theatres. He has performed similar services for the University of Lethbridge Fine Arts Centre, the Arden Theatre (St. Albert), Moyse Hall at McGill University, and the Centre of Film and Theatre at York University. A member of the Associated Designers of Canada, the Canadian Institute of Theatre Technology, and the United States Institute of Theatre Technology, Mr. Silver is a faculty member of the Department of Theatre, York University.

WILLIAM HUTT AND *THE MERRY WIVES OF WINDSOR*

During the summer of 1977, I was doing a 'designer's audition tour,' showing my portfolio to various artistic directors across the country and I had arranged some interviews in Stratford. My first interview was with Robin Phillips, then the Artistic Director of the Stratford Festival. Robin's work had increased the international profile of the company and I had been impressed by the importance he gave to using the visual aspects of his productions to enhance the story-telling. Our interview went well, but I left with no sense of what the results might be. Six weeks later I received an invitation to design for the Stratford Festival's 1978 Season.*

I had visited the Stratford Shakespearean Festival during the early 1960s as a theatre student, and since then as my professional schedule permitted. I had always been impressed by the careful balance of

---

* Another interview was with William Hutt, in his capacity as the Artistic Director of Theatre London, whose winter season still gave him time to continue his onstage work at Stratford. I later was invited to design three productions in the 1978-79 Theatre London season, including *Kiss Me, Kate*, the production which was to be directed by Bill to open the newly-renovated Grand Theatre.

production values - acting, directing, and design - all serving the text, expanding it, enlivening it, enlightening it. Consequently when the Festival invited me to design a production, I was pleased that my own work had grown, in the regional theatres of Canada, to the point that Stratford would be interested in me. But I also had some fears about the challenges of designing at a 'national' institution, the difficulties of design for the thrust stage, and the immensity of the organization required for production of props, scenery, and costumes. I also felt trepidation about even attempting to design in that same arena where Moiseiwitsch, Heeley, Dare, Jackson, and others had set such high standards.

The production was to be *The Merry Wives of Windsor*, to be directed by Peter Moss. The proposed cast list included Domini Blythe and Jennifer Phipps as the 'wives' Mistress Ford and Mistress Page, Alan Scarfe and Lewis Gordon as Ford and Page, and Mary Savidge as Mistress Quickly, with other roles taken by Bob Baker, Jennifer Dale, Maurice Good, Bernard Hopkins, Bill Needles, Barry MacGregor, Richard MacMillan, Richard Whelan, and Tom Wood. These were all actors whom I had seen onstage or with whom I had worked previously.

But the name on the proposed cast list which commanded most significant attention was William Hutt, who was to be our Falstaff. I had seen and admired Mr. Hutt's work at Stratford since those 1960s visits. I recalled watching some of his most rivetting performances - Pandarus in *Troilus and Cressida*, Richard II, Gaev in *The Cherry Orchard*, and Volpone. All these reminded me that the centre of this production would be an actor of tremendous talent, versatility, and experience.

Peter Moss and I began our discussions in October of 1977, first acknowledging both the strengths and weaknesses of the play itself. While *Merry Wives* has continued to be performed regularly, it is not one of Shakespeare's most popular works, although it features one of his most popular characters. The Falstaff of this play certainly lacks the depth of characterization that is seen in the histories. Peter expressed the concern that we should find an appropriate setting of time and place in which to tell the story, as we needed to strengthen the audiences' view of Falstaff as being an anachronism in a changing world. He felt that if we did not achieve this effectively, the play would be reduced to a series of sadistic tricks played on a very sad old man, a one-gag evening.

As I read and reread the play, I understood Peter's concerns. It seemed that the accepted image of a jovial Sir John Falstaff, combined with the commerical value of a good title - *The **Merry** Wives of Windsor* - raised an audience's expectation of continual mirth, while the play itself actually deals with some darker issues, including Ford's tremendous jealousy.

We felt that the production clearly needed to set Falstaff apart from most of the world of the play, and certainly from the two families, the Pages and the Fords. The play is somewhat unique in that there is no person of royalty and the only aristocrat (if one can use the term) is Sir John himself. This play is one of the few in which Shakespeare writes about truly ordinary people. The concerns of the major characters are those of the middle class. Ford and Page are representatives of the merchant class, the bourgeoisie, a class that was gaining social and economic importance during Shakespeare's life. They would have little use for the blustering of a former soldier and adventurer, even if he had been effective at those activities. His supposed court connections have no value in this world. Falstaff and his cronies - Pistol, Nym, and Bardolph (also revived from the history plays) - are remnants of a bygone era, and not very impressive ones at that!

(In this regard, I remember a moment during the rehearsals when Barry MacGregor, playing Pistol, showed me a footnote in one of the editions of the play. Pistol uses a number of unusual words and phrases that any actor would find difficult to make relevant. The footnote suggested that Pistol's words were incomprehensible anachronisms even in Shakespeare's time. And Barry, as always an actor concerned with audience reaction, lamented, 'So what chance do I have with today's audience?')

In preparation for our meetings, Peter Moss had narrowed the field of possible periods in which we might set the production. It seemed clear that the world of this play was not the world of Falstaff of the histories; there are no references to *current* wars or battles. We could set the play in Elizabethan period, as some productions have done, but we felt that we would not have opportunities to show Falstaff as 'from another era.' Although we discussed a Victorian setting, we kept returning to the mid-17th century as a favoured choice. This period would allow us to characterize Falstaff and his group as the seedy remnants of the last great flamboyant 'Cavalier' period, adrift in the business-oriented, somewhat sober, middle-class early Restoration society. A clear delineation was therefore possible in the costuming, emphasizing the differences which

Peter and I agreed were important. This decided, I began the series of sketches, plans, and models that would lead to our production the following summer.

The set was to be a modification of the well-known Stratford stage. The balcony would remain in place, but the pillars would be increased in size, as rough hewn oak posts, and extended to support a thatched roof over the balcony. This 'street-scene' provided the basic background for all our Windsor scenes, interiors and exteriors. The interiors were further characterized by appropriate furniture and lighting. The final act, in the forest, saw the posts open and branches of oak leaves grow to extend over the stage, obscuring the thatch and becoming 'Herne's Oak.'

I began rough costume sketches for the various characters in the play, and as Falstaff was the centre of the play, Falstaff 'concepts' were first to be fully developed on the drawing board.

The very name 'Falstaff' brings with it images and connotations of productions past, as well as the references in both *Merry Wives* and the histories. Falstaff is, to put it bluntly, 'fat.' He refers to himself as 'a mountain.' Previous productions have visually stressed the *roundness* of the old soldier. My first problem was to reconcile these references and images with the physique of the actor cast in this production.

Bill Hutt is a tall man, and much of his bulk is in his chest. His face is more long than round. It would have been far easier to make Bill look thin! The approach that I suggested, and with which Peter agreed, was that if we tried to make Bill look round, we would eventually fail, as padding and other devices would be difficult to blend into his own neck and face area. I was not very keen on massive facial appliances to add latex roundness to Bill's face, thereby limiting his facial expressions, which, after all, are some of what audiences pay to enjoy!

Our approach, therefore, was to concentrate on the image of the *faded* soldier/adventurer. We imagined a Falstaff who might once have been in reasonably good shape, but on whom the combined effects of age and ale had now taken their toll. The muscles had sagged and the beer-belly had grown. Peter and I agreed that our Falstaff was to be more pear-shaped than round, and this was a shape which we could integrate successfully with Bill's physique. Discussions with Bill confirmed his agreement with this approach.

For this production, Falstaff had seven primary costumes, with some minor variations in certain scenes. His basic look was to be the 'cavalier' style - wide-brimmed, plumed hats; wide collar, slashed-sleeve jerkins; full-legged breeches; high boots with wide cuffs; and an off-the-shoulder look to his cape - all 'broken down' to show the effects of age and Falstaff's reduced income. Only in the scenes of his courting the wives did Falstaff make any acknowledgement of current trends in fashion, by wearing the much be-ribboned, heavily buttoned cassock of the later 17th century, complete with a large sash from his right shoulder ending in an exuberant bow at his left hip. The sketch of this costume, nicknamed 'Sir John in Love,' remains one of my favourites.

For the scene in which Falstaff tells of his near-drowning in the basket dumped into the river, the primary costume was the blanket in which Falstaff wrapped himself, but occasionally audiences might catch glimpses of muddied, damp stockings, chemise, and underpants.

In another attempt to flee from discovery at Mr. Ford's, Falstaff disguises himself as the 'fat woman of Brentford,' Mistress Ford's supposed aunt. My joy at designing this costume was to imagine something that the Windsor wives might create from items that would be immediately available in their homes, but would be inadequate as a real disguise for someone of Falstaff's size.

Falstaff's last major costume was his garb 'as Herne the Hunter,' draped in cape and topped with stag's horns. In this, we assumed that Falstaff had made this disguise (as per the wives' instructions) with such seriousness that the result became comical.

Once the designs were completed, fabrics were purchased and even before rehearsals began, initial fittings were taking place. Normally, costumes are based on measurements of the actor's body; in this case, we had to first concentrate on the differences between Bill Hutt's body and our image of Falstaff's body. The Head Cutter for the Festival, Cynthia MacLennan, was to build and/or supervise the making of all Bill's costumes for this production. She and I began with the problem of designing and building a padding suit that would smoothly integrate with Bill's body in areas such as the neck, the arms, and the legs. Since Falstaff is likely to do some rather vigorous moves when pursued by Mr. Ford, or a lot of collapsing into armchairs, I was very adamant that, under the costumes, the padding should move like flesh and fat, not fibre and stuffing. We were also concerned about the warmth of the many layers of costume and padding. Given all these demands, Cynthia created a splendid garment - an open-weave fabric base, similar to long underwear, onto which were sewn small silk bags, in the shape of crescent moons. The bags were filled with stuffing and stitched onto the mesh only along the upper edge (the crescent), with each bag overlapping ones adjacent and below, like shingles on a roof. The so-called 'fat suit' was built out to the required size and when completed allowed Bill to move freely, with the padding creating the same folds and bulges that one would expect in real flesh, no matter what position the actor took. Once we (including Bill) were all satisfied that the shape was right, Cynthia measured the resulting physique, Bill plus the fat suit, and construction could begin of the costumes themselves.

At various stages in the building of a costume, the actor is called in for a 'fitting,' an opportunity to try on the work to date for fit, for look, and for function. At Stratford, fittings are potentially very stressful. Those present for a fitting include the actor, the designer, the cutter, the 'first hand,' the milliner, the bootmaker, possibly the jeweller, and occasionally the director. The costume is put onto the actor layer by layer, with each layer being adjusted as required. Copious notes are made for further work and then each layer is removed, after having been marked for additional adjustments.

Often actors come to the fitting straight from rehearsal, which may have had its own stresses. At Stratford, the repertory system is such that an actor can go from a rehearsal as 'King Lear' into a fitting as 'Feste' and back into rehearsal as 'Capulet.'

It is an accepted truth (though never scientifically proven) amongst those who work backstage that when an actor is unhappy with the development of a role in rehearsal, the manifestations are often first seen in concerns about props, set, or costumes, those physical things with which the actor and the character make contact. Complaints about costumes, of course, are most likely to surface in the fitting. The popular mythology of the theatre is full of stories about 'stars' shredding 'unsatisfactory' costumes or tongue-lashing all in sight, including the designer.

I found myself approaching my first fitting with Mr. Hutt (as the callboard says) with some trepidation. What if the scheme didn't work as well on the body as it did on the sketch pad? What if he'd had a bad day in rehearsals? What if...?

Of course, my fears were unnecessary. At all the fittings, Bill Hutt was patient, even under difficult circumstances. It usually took half an hour to get the padding on and adjusted before we could try the actual character costumes intended for the fitting. While we never attempted to do all Falstaff's costumes in one fitting, we usually tried to do two. This meant Bill was on his feet, in the fat suit, for at least one-and-a-half to two hours, while others buzzed around him, marking, pinning in, letting out, ripping seams, and so on. Through this Bill remained patient. He was very helpful in explaining some stage business that might be affected by the costume; for example, he might require more room in the sleeve for an arm gesture. He was gently emphatic on details that he felt might work against the character he was building in rehearsals. We shared new ideas about Falstaff's clothing, building on the understandings that he, Peter, and I had achieved months before. I was very pleased with the process and with the result.

I have two other particular reminiscences of Bill Hutt in that production. One relates to his skill as an actor who makes full use of the text; the other is his talent as inspired improviser.

The *Oxford English Dictionary*, in one of its myriad editions, is an often-used resource for anyone working on a Shakespeare. A word is defined in all its nuances, and the dates are given when particular implications or meanings were in vogue. Thus, one can see that in Shakespeare's time a word may have had two or three meanings or inferences, and since then other layers of meaning have been added, which colour the word for contemporary audiences.

During one of our final rehearsals for *Merry Wives*, I was able to divert my attention a little from the sets, costumes, props, and lighting which were my responsibility, and return again to the words of the script, now brought to life by the cast. In Act Three, Scene Five, Falstaff describes to Mr. Ford (disguised as Master Brooke) the various indignities which he has endured at the hands of the wives. As I sat in the theatre, I became aware that Bill Hutt was giving astonishingly full value to each word, through his inflections or his gestures, providing us with a touch of each meaning or inference the O.E.D. might offer for any given word. I have since observed Bill's ability to 'milk' the text in some other productions on which we've worked, including *Henry VIII* at Stratford in 1986 especially when he delivered Cardinal Wolsey's farewell.

My second reminiscence is of the photocall for *Merry Wives*. The Stratford Festival souvenir programme deadlines often demand that photos be taken of productions early in the rehearsal process - indeed, in some cases, before rehearsals have really begun. The *Merry Wives* photocall took place several weeks into the rehearsal period, but only some costumes, props, and set pieces were completed specially for the occasion. Peter Moss had chosen scenes that might make good photo material and I had worked to have available the items required for those scenes. Robert Ragsdale, the veteran photographer of many of Canada's greatest theatre events, was assigned to the production.

One of the photos was to be a 'moment' that in fact never happened in the play, but was too good to pass up. The scene was the Garter Inn, represented by a heavy oak table, some stools, and Falstaff's large armchair. On the table, some goblets, a flagon of wine, and a plate of what was supposed to be 'capon,' most likely acquired earlier in the day from the local Kentucky Fried Chicken outlet. The actors were Mary Savidge as Mistress Quickly and Bill Hutt as Falstaff. As Robert Ragsdale started shooting with each of the various cameras hanging from his neck, Mary and Bill started the dialogue from a Quickly/Falstaff scene; however, as more photos were required to get the 'right shot' and as Shakespeare's words had run out, the inspiration of the moment overcame Bill and Mary. They launched into a remarkably funny sequence of wordplay along with improvisation based on pieces of chicken. The audience, consisting of the other actors and the entire production staff, were reduced to tears, and as Robert Ragsdale kept shooting, Bill and Mary, Falstaff and Mistress Quickly, traded improvised pseudo-Shakespearean one-liners. I believe the image of those fleeting moments will remain my fondest memory of *The Merry Wives of Windsor.*

Copyright: Phillip Silver 1994

MERVYN BLAKE

After training at the Royal Academy of Dramatic Art, Mervyn Blake (b. 1907) made his professional début at London's Embassy Theatre in 1933, and later was a member of the Stratford-upon-Avon Company from 1952 to 1955. He worked with many of the 'greats' in English theatre - Laurence Olivier, Vivien Leigh, Anthony Quayle, Michael Redgrave, Edith Evans, and Peggy Ashcroft - and moved to Canada in 1957. One of the most beloved character actors at the Stratford Festival, he has appeared in every play in the Shakespearean canon. The recipient of two (unsolicited) Tyrone Guthrie Awards, a Dora Mavor Moore Award (Saturday, Sunday, Monday), *and the Queen's Jubilee Medal, he is the first actor to be honoured with a seat in his name in all three Stratford, Ontario, theatres.*

THREE LEARS

All three of his Lears were marvellous. His last one - for Robin Phillips in 1988 at the Third Stage, was very good, indeed. Being in a small theatre, you began to feel that it was a man's mental reflections which had come out not in big passionate things but in much more controlled ones. Not all of it did I agree with. I didn't like the 'Never, never, never, never, never.' That disappointed me. But Robin is inclined to scale everything down in production. He wants you to speak in whispers, if necessary, to capture feeling. And it's always as if there's a camera at the back of his mind, taking in all the inner thoughts.

I would say that Robin's production was last in my order of preference. Bill wanted to do something different from the other Lears he'd done. I think some of the best performances of Lear I saw was on the 1961-62 Canadian Players tour with David Gardner's Eskimo *King Lear*. Bill had to deal with contingencies, and if he had to deal with difficulties of staging, he seemed to suddenly bring something out which was magnificent for the occasion. We once played at a huge girls' school in Saratoga, a famous racing town not far from New York. They had quite an inappropriate stage, so we had to quickly find ways of being able to stage the thing. In spite of all the difficulties, Bill managed to give one of the

best performances I've ever seen anyone give. That particular performance equalled any of the big performances of Lear that I've ever seen by
Michael Redgrave or other well-known actors. He was absolutely
marvellous. A bundle of girls came around after the show, all of them
crying. I was, in a sense, managing the company at the time while also
acting. I brought this particular girl around to Bill. She was in complete
tears. She had wanted to ask for his autograph but couldn't. She just burst
into tears and couldn't stop. All of us backstage began to be a bit wet too.
Bill soothed her, 'My dear girl, it's all right, it's all right. Do you want
my signature? I'll give it to you. Please don't cry.'

Some parts of the 1972 *Lear* that David William directed, and in which
I played Kent, were absolutely magnificent. Bill was a *king* giving away
his kingdom - but with magnanimity, and he was not to be betrayed. I
think the end fell down a bit, in comparison with what he had started
with, but in general I think it was his best Lear.

I always compare him with Michael Redgrave because Bill is as close
to Michael Redgrave, whom I knew very well and acted with, as anyone
can be. In his looks, height, delivery. In a single season, Michael could
give some of the worst performances and some of the most brilliant
you've ever seen a famous actor give. Bill, too, was very up and down in
his performances. He was extremely good, however, at gauging audiences and sensing different atmospheres on the European tour. You
could tell when he was playing a scene how he felt about the mood of the
audience at the time, and he was generally accurate. Olivier could do that
- he would sniff an audience - without your even knowing that he was
doing it. Bill is not that kind of tiger, but he does gauge an audience very
well. I don't know how he did it, but whenever he'd die in my arms, I
always sensed when he was playing the scene slightly differently.

MAURICE GOOD

Maurice Good has had a distinguised forty-year theatre career encompassing acting for the Dublin Gate and Abbey Theatres, the Old Vic and Theatre Workshop companies, in London's West End, Paris, Berlin, the Middle East, and with most leading theatres throughout Canada and America. Since settling in Canada, he has appeared frequently in major roles with the Stratford Festival and is the author of Every Inch A Lear *(Sono Nis Press). His celebrated solo programmes include* John Synge Comes Next *(OUP),* Under Ben Bulben *(about Yeats), and* The Ham in Sam *(about Beckett). He has written and acted extensively for radio, television, and film in Ireland, the U.K., and Canada* (Moby Dick, The Saint, The Avengers, The Wars, *etc.). His various honours include the John Coffen Literary Award (London University), a Tyrone Guthrie Award (Stratford Festival), and appointment as Associate Professor (Theatre) at Memorial University, Newfoundland. He currently writes, directs, teaches, and pursues film-work on both sides of the Atlantic.*

A PORTABLE SPHINX

A Portrait of William Hutt as the Fool in King Lear
Edited by Maurice Good from his book **Every Inch A Lear: A Journal of Rehearsal** *of the Peter Ustinov/William Hutt/Robin Phillips production at the Stratford Festival, Ontario, 1979.*

INTRODUCTION

It is an enormous honour to be asked to contribute a section to a book celebrating William Hutt's seventy-fifth birthday. The best words, for me the only appropriate words that I can choose, have already been written about him in my *Every Inch A Lear*, published by Sono Nis Press, Victoria, 1982. I say 'best' and 'only appropriate words' because Bill Hutt sent me (early in 1982) the most kind, generous, deeply supportive and encouraging words that I've ever received in a letter - from anyone. I've long lost that letter. But I will never forget nor cease to be moved by his wise and so glowingly encouraging words which helped make a long, long contract in the Blackstone Theatre, Chicago, into a halcyon adventure while I was anxiously awaiting my first author's copy. Bill had (it transpired) bought and as instantly read the first copy sold - a long time before my mailed copies at last caught up with me. But Bill's fan letter (the first I'd ever received for a book in Canada) was more precious to me than any of the enthusiastic press-reviews that came later. Bill's kind and timely words comforted and convinced me that one of the most difficult, demanding, and challenging times of my life had been worked through - to something of a worthwhile result - and that it was time to be getting on to the next main event. The event in this case is now to edit together a celebratory sequence of extracts from *Every Inch A Lear* in the hope that they'll be a worthy offering to Bill's many, many friends, fans, and admirers, and - if I'm lucky - to the remarkable William Hutt himself: a great and generous man and actor.

JOURNAL

There is basic agreement that Lear is dotty at the start, with judgement gone, and the play shows him regaining it. A heading in the Festival Brochure subtitles the production 'the Education of a King.' Physically not up to many challenges, this Lear; which is why, in the opening scene, Ustinov says he may well fall asleep.

Bill Hutt (the previous Lear at Stratford) thinks that the Fool also is 'getting awfully old.' Is the Fool older than Lear? Hutt: 'Very possibly - but we can't *both* be shaking all night.' Ustinov: 'Yes...Boy...do keep still!' Hutt: 'It's only my little finger! *You're* quivering *all* over.'

Phillips, referring to Ustinov's ability to do any accent in the world, wonders about Voice, which 'changes so much depending on who you are.' True. Ustinov promises we'll 'have a smell around that.' Hutt, usually so rotund of voice and presence, is already looking 'terribly thin.'

Turning to Hutt and Ustinov, Phillips says, 'We should find out something about where *these two* are at.' It's apparent very quickly that with these two actors, as Fool and Lear, no joke is ever really going to end. Both achieve, even sitting at the table, an incredible physical alertness in the head. They read the scene (1.iv) again, slowly, each hanging on to the text, like two old dogs worrying at the same bone. They emanate generations of word-game and crossword expertise. And even when the dialogue runs out, they improvise on. Hutt: 'You can't do that one again, we had "Intransigence" *last* week!' Ustinov (with a playful slapping gesture): 'You're my portable Sphinx!'

Hutt and Ustinov both know and share something larger than talent. They share (with Phillips) the responsibility that comes with the privilege of work in this play. They all possess what Kent recognizes in Lear: 'You have that in your countenance which I would fain call master.' 'What's that?' 'Authority.'

Cartoon by Peter Ustinov of William Hutt. Copyright Maurice Good 1982

Later in rehearsal, Bill Hutt emerges from the ruck (of the massed presence of Lear's knights) with that exceptional actor's enormous calculation, for his first line as the Fool: the ruck in this case being not only the presence of so many actors, but their loosely varied responses to Lear's as varied vocalizations. Hutt's empty pocket-lining, pulled out in conical equivalence to a medieval coxcomb, has a more than nineteenth-century ambivalence. His and Peter's first salutation with fluttering fingers - delightful invention - both with their hands raised to the sides of their heads, makes a nice contest each day, to see who'll get what in first. Offering Peter his 'coxcomb,' Bill usually slaps Peter's outstretched hand - an over-greedy reach for forbidden candy. But today Peter beats him to it, hand moved away deftly out of line, and almost smacking Bill's, which is likewise whipped away in a balancing sharpness of reflex. The Lear-Fool exchange continues its dangerously uncharted course, with seventeen actors side-stepping, in contribution to the day's improvised and newly-found jokes. There's a Fool, finally, of course, in any court, as there's one in any cabinet, and rather more in parliaments; but our Fool, and Shakespeare's, is none.

(For the costume rehearsal of 1.iv, the mass entrance and the cry of 'Dinner, Ho! Dinner!' in the courtyard, envelops our stage in the browns and russets of Lear and his knights, who are obstreperous enough to convince us that they are all accustomed to leaving a party room in a terrible state. Poor Goneril! The scene combines a pastoral glow with more than a hint of the dissolute. All tones suggest the Fall, a gentle visual melancholia in these autumnal shades. And, yet, there is a sensation of something ominous, mixed in with the levity and high spirits. Perhaps it's Bill's very tatty green velvet frock-coat. It helps to dominate (as any major role *should* instantly dominate), and is in keeping with the very acid edge of some or almost all of this Fool's first exchanges with Lear.)

In the courtyard scene (1.v), following Lear's self-expulsion from his daughter's home, Lear stands, attended only by the Fool. Two potently evocative figures, they shuffle forward a little. They both have the same walk. Who, I wonder, is watching whom more carefully? The fact is that both characters (and both actors) are operating at maximum sensitivity of peripheral vision and sense. They both look out front as absolutely as two competing variety comics. The duologue proceeds or, rather, tries to, in the early-in-the-day uncertainties, the joint grasping for correct lines attuned to the presence, in each, of the absolutely correct thoughts. It's a halting attempt at comfort from a Fool to a Master who has recognized the folly of being comforted. The totally shared sense of dereliction and isolation is as absolute as in Vladimir and Estragon; my conjecture is immobilized as I realise that both actors can clearly encompass the huge demands of either of those great *Godot* roles. This is the kind of acting I love: perhaps it's in that dimension, most frequently found - and only during rehearsals - that our audiences can never witness. It's the very breath of Beckett.

There's time, afterwards, for a brief chat. 'I'm not *quite* right on the lines there - but *almost* right,' claims Peter Ustinov cheekily. Bill Hutt, typically, preserves his very reserved, smiling silence. He's done Lear twice already, and I often wonder about how many of the lines *he* can still remember. Probably more than Peter has, yet, managed to memorize. (Or myself, as Ustinov's Standby - but trusting I'll never have to go on in coming performances!)

They have another go. Hutt's Fool attempts his patter of consolation, each of his lines becomes a fresh beginning in distraction; and Lear, embedded in his guilt and unease, is unable - or incapable - of being distracted or consoled. It really is very like that discussion of the two old Beckett tramps on the theoretic proposition of hanging (as a way out for one of them), which they at last abandon - only because of a technical difficulty - in the absence of reliable props in their empty landscape. It gives me a feeling of interminable sporadic exchanges by two aging brothers from adjoining beds far into the night, on themes worn smooth by variations since they were boys. Ustinov, in the broken, unfinished line - 'I did her wrong...' - startles me, as I'd always thought that Lear was thinking of Cordelia here. And yet, it could be related to either of his other daughters, or perhaps even his wife - all we know of her in the play is that she is dead, and has presumably been dead for a long time. Hutt looks up to the stars with the conjecture of a Captain Boyle, and finds there the hard truth he's been looking for - as well as the *light* that a great actor quite constantly, if finally unconsciously, always finds on stage. The Fool's line, 'Thou shoulds't not have been old till thou hads't been wise,' is one that Lear does not want to hear, one (the way Bill does it) that we do not want to hear ourselves. We hear it often this morning, as the scene is taken again and again, as Bill continues to explore this (and his other lines) with an increasingly desolate emphasis.

Phillips (using his own small dimmer-board) takes the stage lights out to total darkness. His cigarette is the only glow in the black. '*Outside acting* is very weird,' he says, 'let's go again in the dark.' And the words from Bill and Peter flutter out to us again: contained, locked forever, each one of them in the passing instant of each word's delivery. Like leaves, they fall as interminably, as inexorably, as the cadences of Beckett's tramps, confirming again the genesis, the origin, of Sam's so special species. Phillips pursues the theme of economy in the voice, pursuit being possible because of the veteran techniques of vocal ease from two masters of their craft. It's often better to use a little less than too much. Not that the words must be frozen forever into a murmur, but, rather, that the issue is never to push the sound towards any unnecessary extras.

The scene is done again, once more in the dark, the voices of Hutt and Ustinov finding the words, caressing them, and finally releasing them. And their pauses also assume an equal power with the words. The silence in great dramatic writing is as potent as the sound. The thoughts of Lear and his Fool run on in the silences between them, as absolutely as the music moves on in the rests of Mozart or Beethoven. The scene ends once more; there is a long, thoughtful pause. From everyone. The lights come back on.

In III.ii - the 'Blow winds and crack your cheeks' scene - Bill Hutt gradually makes his way downstage, settling for an attempt at shelter in a crouching huddle, a foetal bundle, absolutely down-centre at Peter's feet. It takes him a while to arrive there during Peter's arias, and he does it with economy, suggesting in his very bent stance the full ferocity of the gale. We now have a wind-machine off-stage, for I can hear its roar, and Lear and the Fool face us with hair and shirt-tails and trousers flapping. On the exit, Peter somewhat pre-empts Bill's dance as the Fool, becoming almost amiable. They sing their way off-stage - accepting the odds against them - as we all choose, often, to sing in adversity. Both clap arms to armpits; Peter cavorts like a Fool, Bill walks like Lear. They have almost switched roles.

In III.vi, 'Gloucester's Barn' or the 'hovel scene,' the stage is bare except for the wind-swept figures of Lear, Fool, Kent, and Edgar (entering now as 'Poor Tom'). They are begrimed, wet, and exhausted, and mime their crouching entrance from the storm outside. But - not quite four! One of the quartet is missing. Bill Hutt, entering, solo, from the wrong side, momentarily lost, is apologetic. 'Sorry. In my script - I'd marked it down - it says "Enter Stage Left".' Bill Hutt, the veteran of uncountable years at Stratford, and as many starring roles, so many of them here on this Avon stage, is delightedly reminded by many of us that 'stage left' is indeed where the others came on. Just as delightedly, Bill concurs, 'Why - so it is!' 'Never mind,' Robin consoles him, 'Happens all the time to our new juveniles.'

As they move into the darkness of the wings to try the entrance once more, Ustinov can be heard, lightheartedly: 'I'll talk a word with this same *learned* Thespian.' He clouts Bill affectionately on his disordered ample locks. Bill *has* an academic look, excellent casting for professors. He would be the very last to describe himself as 'learned' - yet he is so. A near half-century of grappling (with his intrinsic relaxation) onto so many major roles equips him beautifully for this Fool. This unique Fool is a powerful cumulative contribution to this production, to be learned from by all of our juveniles - aged or no.

The wind machine is tremendous, but Hutt projects cleanly over the din. He is using the moment to look more doomed than Lear, his Fool becoming, in facial expression, an evocation of every insomniac's dawn.

His last line has a valedictory cadence, 'And - I'll go to bed at noon,' delivered into the half-sleeping face of an old man as vulnerable and important, as the old are so seldom, regrettably, to any of us.

THE PHOTOCALL

The Photocall is well-advanced. Stage and stalls are engulfed in activity, the full cast is in costume; there's a full back-stage technical crew, entire Stage Management, all costume and wig people, publicity and PR departments, dressers, photographers, and me. It's like a major sound-stage at MGM and Robin Phillips, exhaustively himself, is prima donna of it all. He is everywhere.

Phillips sets up some solos for Peter, then Bill. With flying iron-grey hair, unkempt in creased greasy green velvet frock-coat, Hutt looks as if he's stepped out of a Franz Hals solo-portrait; archaic, a discovered Dorian Gray seemingly saying, 'Oh, well - just for you, old friend - I'll try to make an impression.' When an effect is so totally imagined, as Bill has so absolutely imagined it - the full costume merely a last added bonus - there's no question of trying for impression. Fulsome fact of character is already there. Guaranteed from the first day of rehearsal - when we were introduced to an already enveloping mane of actor's locks. Bill's hair has since developed into the final amplitude of the wild hair of the legendary hag of Beare.

They've moved onto the next picture set-up. Bill and Peter are swapping gags, relaxing from the exigencies of the real (and often still elusive) lines of the text, they now try some of their own. Bill: 'Now then - keep a Seville tongue in your head.' 'A ha! You fell into that one.' 'So will you, boy, every night.'

And now, we've a set-up for the storm scenes. Robin is wetting everyone down with a hand spray. He calls for wind and smoke, and the wind-machine transforms the belching wraiths into an appearance of horizontally driven rain. Loose strips of scarf stream in the gale from Peter's and Bill's shoulders. Above the roar of the blades, Peter, now in much broken-down browns, bootless, breaks into snatches of Wagner. He's very much like Ustinov should look in such a role. He's Every Inch a Lear. Robin dodges in and out of smoke and wind to add more spray to Peter's hands, neck, beard, cheeks, and glistening brow.

Suddenly, the foreground is galvanized into activity as a score of hands manipulate a huge black plastic covering over the fore-stage, extending to the steps of the upper platform. All seems set for some *pièce de résistance*. Two large children's wading pools appear from nowhere, one of them weathered, the other brand-new and iridescent with Donald Ducks, Snoopys, Mickey Mouses. The moment gleams with anticipation. 'Oh,' (from Peter), 'for our second childhood!' 'There's one for you, too,' gloats Hutt as the spanking new one is set down before the steps at Peter's feet. 'My turn for the pail!' howls Peter in childhood tantrum. 'Now - you're not going to start on that one!' wails Bill with matching belligerence.

And, with that, a six-foot ladder materializes beside the kiddie-pool, and Robin is climbing to its top with a very large - and full - watering can. 'Now, then, you two!' Everyone crowds forward to the front of the stage, from the wings and the stalls as, with wind-machine roaring, our two most eminent and senior Company actors step down for baptism into the bright round bath. 'Fine,' says Robin, 'let's have it from "Rumble thy bellyful!,"' and starts to pour. Hilarity rises amongst the Company as Peter and Bill are deluged in an unremittent downpour. And Peter's lines are stopped, literally, in the mouth by the channelling streams. 'Spout!...Rain,' he splutters, 'I tax you not, you watering-can, with unkindness...Then let fall your horrible "waters."' He gulps it out - and some of it in - valiantly finishing to a sustained round of applause.

As our two distinguished actors stand like especially naughty children, soaked in their Sunday clothes, Robin quickly gets a refill. And more than a dozen actors in turn are urgently insisting to me: 'Maurice - you've got to get this one!' Alas, I'm without a camera, though no mere photograph could do justice to this event. Happily, however, Peter later offers a contribution, a 'retrospective cartoon,' which may yet celebrate the occasion.

As Robin, replenished, ascends his ladder for the reprise, Peter, always ready with the most apposite quote from *Lear*, calls up to him, 'Nature's above Art, in this respect.' And we have yet another replay, as Peter and Bill, sodden to their squelching shoes, play the sequence under the renewed shower with delighted abandon. 'Oh! Oh, Oh! 'tis FOUL!' finishes Peter, with an emphasis he'll never dare to forget in performance. The final drops fall from Robin's can. Peter, shuffling with some knee-clutching, asks in a small voice, 'Can I go to the toilet now?' And Bill, boldly relaxed, adds, 'I have.'

The Photocall continues. But I go. There isn't anything left that can follow that.

(And there still isn't! Happy birthday, dear Bill! We have all learned, and are learning still, from all your superb example! Thank you, always.)

CHRISTOPHER NEWTON

After his first great theatrical epiphany - Tyrone Guthrie's Edwardian production of Troilus and Cressida *at the Old Vic - Christopher Newton (b. 1936) decided on a professional career that led him from Leeds to a North American journey of discoveries. Various apprenticeships in Theatre Departments and playhouses carried him as an actor to the Stratford Festival in the sixties, and from there to his eventual career as director and artistic director at Theatre Calgary, the Vancouver Playhouse, and then the Shaw Festival. His leadership of the Shaw has spanned more than a decade, establishing him as perhaps the most successful artistic director in Canada, and his directorial achievements - particularly with productions of* Major Barbara, Heartbreak House, You Never Can Tell, Man and Superman, Pygmalion, *and* Cavalcade - *have stamped him as a director of ambitious scope, vision, and vitality. His Shavian productions have succeeded in making Shaw seem startlingly contemporary and sexy.*

INSTINCTIVE RESPONSES

I think that what I like best about Bill's work is the listening - the silence that is alive and always curiously dangerous. I remember two moments from *Man and Superman* at The Shaw. The first is at the opening of the play: Roebuck Ramsden reading a book with a red cover. He is seated at a desk, centre stage, facing the audience. Everything is silvery and very stark. The playing area is defined by two very thin, plain, white proscenium arches which focus the eye on some geometrically arranged chairs and the desk. Behind the desk, in a pale dressing gown, a silver-haired figure, holding the red book in a manner which, without movement, nevertheless lets us know that he hates it. Or is it actually the manner in which the book is held that tells us what is going on? After all, hands and book simply rest on the empty white desk. Look again. It seems very ordinary and yet we sense something dangerous in the stillness. Something is about to happen, something that might be a surprise. We are on edge. The reading continues. The book is still held on the table, but now another emotion has begun to unfold. There is now a sense of distress. A page is turned. This is the only sound: the sharp flutter of paper. The reading continues. Suddenly the book is closed and dropped into the waste-paper basket.

How does an actor achieve any of this? Well, I don't really know for sure, but I think that this connection of actor to audience is rather like the sensation that will cause me to look around, convinced that someone is watching. In its most complex form, I can look across a room and fall in love. An actor uses these energies. Whatever they are, however hard to describe, they are nonetheless quite real. The greater the actor, the more complex the manipulation of the connection. Without actually doing anything other than thinking, a great actor can change the tone of a scene.

Bill is able to do this.

My second memory - from *Man and Superman* - is from the *Don Juan in Hell* sequence. Bill as Roebuck Ramsden also plays the Statue. He takes fourth place to Don Juan, the Devil, and even to Donna Anna, but he provides a crucial element of the plot in this sequence. Bill sits at the long table that stretches from the back of the stage almost to the footlights. His costume is seventeenth century. He sports a full bottomed wig and looks a little like engravings of Daniel Defoe. He is close to the audience and playing with a glass. Michael Ball as Don Juan (John Tanner) is talking. It's a long, complicated speech. My eye wanders to Bill at the front of the stage, back to Michael moving round the table, and I realize that simply by the manner in which he is listening, Bill is supporting Don Juan's argument. There's a delicate turn of the head and adjustment of the wig - after all, he is in the most powerful position. The turn concentrates my attention on Don Juan. I can't remember if I blocked that wig adjustment. Probably not. It feels like an actor's instinctive response to a moment. What is remarkable is the delicacy and, above all, the generosity.

I can't really ever remember talking to Bill about my ideas on acting. I would suggest that his approach, in his own mind, is always extremely practical. He will say: "To get the laugh I will need to do this." "This" can be anything from a pause to a gesture to a sharp movement of the whole body. He has an innate sense of the theatrical, and I have no memory of him being wrong when it comes to the practicalities of the theatre.

He's sometimes wrong in tone. I've seen him grab a laugh which he has no business getting because it hurts something later in the play. I've seen him be quite crude - again in pursuit of a laugh. But I suspect that these faults were noticeable because the director didn't challenge him.

I was nervous, at first, directing Bill. After all, he is one of the few theatrical personalities whom I have always admired. As a very new, wet-behind-the-ears actor in Toronto in the early sixties, I saw his quirky, dangerous Eskimo Lear in a tiny theatre that used to exist behind the corner of Bloor and Yonge. I remember, thirty years later, the presence, the odd gait, the swoop of the voice, the immediacy. My nervousness as a director disappeared quite quickly because he took it for granted that I knew what I was doing. I tend to build up scenes from the details of conversation and action, and Bill seemed to like this. It's only later that I can sense a shape. By then I'd gained his trust so that I could alter the rhythms without disturbing the character.

Another memory. A reversal. In October 1968 I started Theatre Calgary. That summer I was at Stratford. I had determined to take out to Calgary as many of the younger Stratford actors as I could afford. Ken Welsh, Eric Donkin, Neil Munro, Jimmy Blendick, Mary Hitch, Ann Anglin - all came out. It was exciting for us. We had our own theatre at last. The third production was to be *Gaslight*. Kenny Welsh and Eric Donkin who were doing *The Odd Couple* and a modern dress version of Ben Jonson's *The Alchemist* were to play Mr. Manningham and the detective. I was to direct. Late in the season at Stratford, there was a change in the following year's schedule. Jean Gascon found me in the Avon Bar. He had just taken over and was perhaps a touch nervous. He was certainly pretty overbearing. 'You cannot have Ken. I have him in something else.' 'But he's signed. It's all announced.' 'Then you must make a change. This is a *Big* theatre. You have a very *Little* theatre. That's how things work.'

It was as if all the sound had suddenly stopped in the bar. I walked away from Jean to a far corner. I remember Martha Henry coming over and saying, 'What on earth's happened to you?' Moments later Bill came over. 'Something's happened. What is it?' Both of them had been putting up with my primal, theatrical enthusiasms all summer. I told them. Bill said: 'All right, this is what you do. Call Jean Roberts at the Canada Council. Tell her what's happened. Get some money for my airfare and I'll come out and direct *Gaslight* and you can play Mr. Manningham.'

And that's what happened.

When he was in Calgary, he took a suite at the Palliser and he played the visiting star to the hilt. He appeared on every talk show in town. Pat

Armstrong got him interviews with every paper in Alberta. And on every talk show and in every interview he promoted Theatre Calgary and our little gang of young, green actors who had more enthusiasm than knowledge or money. On top of this, Bill - and it was only his second directing job - gave us a wonderful *Gaslight*, full of odd insights, all held together with a wiry, edgy, suspenseful tension.

Such generosity, such practicality, such knowledge, such talent, and such friendship is rare.

HERBERT WHITTAKER

The leading Canadian newspaper theatre critic of his day, Herbert Whittaker (b. 1910) has been an important voice in the country. He was instrumental in promoting the Dominion Drama Festival, the Stratford and Shaw Festivals, the National Arts Centre, and various other theatrical causes. He retired from the Globe and Mail *in 1975, but has continued to keep abreast of developments here and abroad. Among his numerous distinctions are two honorary D.Litt degrees (1971 and 1993), the Toronto Drama Bench Award (1975), and the Order of Canada (1976).*

AWARENESS OF HIS WORTH

At seventy-five, William Hutt still has a way to go before he reaches Gielgudian heights of national acclaim, but in terms of Canada's stage development I think we can safely say his ascent has been remarkable indeed. He has proved, as have none other of our major actors, that a theatrical career starting off in summer stock can soar to stardom in our two national and classical theatres. He has represented us abroad - in Russia and Australia, no less - and held his own opposite such notable international players as Sir John Gielgud, Dame Maggie Smith, Jessica Tandy, and Sir Peter Ustinov. The Governor-General has honoured him and, more than that, Hutt won the approval of Noel Coward himself.

At home, his competition has been fierce. John Colicos set the standard for Lear at the Stratford Festival with a demanding monarch full of passion. Christopher Plummer, glittering with wicked charm, staked out Hamlet and Cyrano de Bergerac for himself. Hutt was challenged by such unique visitors as Paul Scofield and Frederick Valk, and by Douglas Campbell and Tony van Bridge, following some of them in important roles. Only Douglas Rain, whose work is perhaps more often flawless, stands up to Hutt in Stratford's annals.

But of them all, Hutt shows the greatest self-concern, awareness of his worth, and ambition to establish this worth on his home territory. That ambition has driven him onward and upward to the heights - more slowly, perhaps, than the competition but undeniably.

As a theatre critic from the half-century mark, I have watched him and been mightily impressed. Yet I worry that I did not give this accomplished actor the full credit for versatility that perhaps I should. Why is this? Am I not known for generosity towards actors of talent?

I think, on the whole, that I made the mistake of characterizing him as a high comedian - a rare one in the theatre of my days. We had low comics and middle comedians (many of the latter feminine), but few enough high comedians. And William Hutt, with his air of aloofness, of I-don't-give-a-damnedness, his spot-on timing, was a comedian worthy of Noel Coward's approval - which he had, incidentally, when making one of his few excursions into the West End.

Perhaps I also became aware of that thin edge of pomposity in his loftier roles. When Hutt turned serious, he knew the personal risks. (In Keith Garebian's biography of him, he is quoted as resenting anybody who is more pompous than himself - a joke that suggests an ability to find deeper layers of self-awareness than most actors indulge in.) He didn't seem to have the extraordinary knack of Laurence Olivier, who protected himself from loftiness with his comic instincts ever on the ready. Olivier could find comedy of some sort or other in every part he played - Macbeth, Coriolanus, Captain Edgar. Yet, I suggest, he was not a greater comedian than is our William Hutt.

Could the difference between Olivier and Hutt lie in their audiences' expectations? The British are known for their ability to find humour in stones, to wit in everything. We Canadians are a more orderly lot, dividing our comedy and our tragedy into proper categories of enjoyment. If that generality is not false, I see William Hutt as the people's man. He is an actor who is capable of excellence in high comedy and in low, in high tragedy and low melodrama, in low Shakespeare (I remember his Froth) and in high (his Innuit Lear was perhaps his best), in Gogol, Molière, Coward, and Pinero as in Albee, O'Neill, and Chekhov. He can play them all as required.

William Hutt is indeed the most Canadian of the eminent and talented players of his day. His seventy-fifth birthday should plainly be declared a national holiday, and he should broadcast the play of his choice over the Canadian Broadcasting Corporation, coast-to-coast.

PATRICIA COLLINS

English-born actress, Patricia Collins has worked extensively in many Toronto theatres, winning two Dora Awards so far for The Europeans *(Necessary Angel Theatre) and* White Biting Dog *(Tarragon). She has given remarkable performances at other leading Canadian theatres, particularly the Stratford Festival, the Grand Theatre, and the National Arts Centre. The recipient of Etrog and Wilderness Awards for film and television work, she played diverse roles in such productions as the* Wojeck *series, CBC's* Lady Windermere's Fan, *and Atom Egoyan's* The Adjuster.

BREWSTER

PLACE: The Grand Theatre, London, Ontario
PLAY: *THE DINING ROOM* by A.R. Gurney
SCENE: A Children's Birthday Party

Four five-year olds are boisterously celebrating. I'm seated next to Brewster, a particularly precocious little boy who wears a bowtie, party hat, and circular horn-rimmed glasses. He fixes me with a leer and whispering in my ear with a child's lisp, proposes a most lascivious deed involving the two of us.

Choking on my party favour and trying valiantly to stay in my own five-year old's character, I look into his eyes and I'm gearing up to deliver some snappy patter. And he's got this twinkle - this gleam, the likes of which I've never seen before. It's a sparkle one associates with very mischievous children, except that this little boy is WILLIAM HUTT and he's sporting a Van Dyke beard and his leonine head is covered with silver and he's 73 years old for God's sake.

Many people have tried to analyse talent, as if it were something scientific and molecular, ripe for dissection like a dead frog on a bed of wax.

Mr. Hutt's talent is inexplicable, except to say that he is a superb observer and this makes him ageless.

There was no doubt in my mind that during that scene he most definitely was five years old and his name was Brewster.

PETER MOSS

Apart from his extensive freelance directing in theatre and television - including credits at the Grand Theatre, the National Arts Centre, CFTO, and ABC - Peter Moss (b. 1947) was Associate Director of the Crewe Repertory Theatre and of the Phoenix Theatre (Leicester) in England, Associate Director of the Stratford Festival (1977-80), and Artistic Director of Young People's Theatre, Toronto (1980-91), where the theatre commissioned, produced, and presented thirty new Canadian plays. Mr. Moss directed two of Timothy Findley's plays for their world premières. He is currently Creative Head, TV Children's Programs, at the CBC.

HOT AND SEXY

Anyone who is lucky enough to call Bill Hutt a friend will acknowledge his warmth, generosity, loyalty, humour, and big-hearted spirit - all qualities that make him a joy to know. But after over fifteen years of working and playing with Bill, I most treasure his capacity to surprise - as happened once again when we were working on Timothy Findley's *The Stillborn Lover* at the Grand Theatre in London.

The scene we were working on was a flashback, where an elderly couple who have lived an extremely rich and complex life together, transform themselves into the young, passionate selves they were on the night they married. It was a very challenging scene for Martha Henry and Bill to play.

Now, Martha, whom I first fell in love with as an actress watching her perform Titania at the Stratford Festival (1968), is one of the most sensuous performers I have ever seen on stage.

But as for Bill, while countless thousands can testify to his magnificent and commanding presence on stage - his range extends from the tragic dignity of the 'greats' (Prospero, Lear, Uncle Vanya) to lustful buffoonery and some truly wild comic performances (*Much Ado About Nothing, The Merry Wives of Windsor, The Imaginary Invalid*). The list of his triumphs is seemingly endless, but 'hot and sexy' were not usually part of his repertoire.

I needn't have been concerned. By the time they were finished, the rehearsal hall was steaming and they had created an incredible scene.

Bill's performance was so convincing that my eighteen year old daughter, whose general taste runs to the young, blond Adonis type, leaned over during a performance of that particular scene and said, 'I could marry him.'

RICHARD MONETTE

An accomplished actor with credits in Canada, Britain, and the United States - including tour de force performances in Hosanna *and* Judgement *and roles such as Romeo, Hamlet, Henry V, Caliban, Parolles, Edmund, and Benedick - Richard Monette (b. 1944) is the first Artistic Director of the Stratford Festival to have been selected from the ranks of its own regular acting company. Winner of a Dora Mavor Moore Award (1991) for Outstanding Direction of* Saint Joan *at Theatre Plus, he has directed productions of* Romeo and Juliet, The Taming of the Shrew, The Comedy of Errors - *all three also filmed for the CBC -* Shirley Valentine, Blake, Come and Go, Much Ado About Nothing, Twelfth Night, *and* Hamlet.

VALENTINE TO A CONSUMMATE ARTIST

My life changed forever one afternoon in 1959, the day I saw my first play at the Stratford Festival. I was 15 years old, and not only was it my first visit to Stratford, it was the first time I'd ever seen a live performance of Shakespeare. The play was *As You Like It*, and the actor playing Jaques was William Hutt.

I remember his performance to this day, for it filled my awestruck sensibilities like a film close-up. Here was an actor who not only captivated me with the sound of Shakespeare's words, he made me understand their sense and the emotion behind them. When he came to the famous soliloquy 'All the world's a stage,' he began it so unselfconsciously and spoke it with such immediacy that we in the audience were completely caught up in what seemed a wholly organic moment in the life of the play. We were thrilled immeasurably by the famous speech without ever being reminded that it *was* a famous speech.

I came away from that performance in love with Stratford, in love with Shakespeare, and in love with acting; and I knew with complete certainty what I wanted to do with my life. I wanted to be an actor, like William Hutt - though I realized even then that to emulate him was to emulate greatness.

Three qualities, perhaps, combine to make a great actor: natural gifts; hard, disciplined labour; and the application of intelligence and intuition. Nature has given Bill a beautiful voice, a voice of vast range and exquisite timbre. I asked him once how he developed such vocal agility, and he replied, 'When I was 13, my voice broke, and it settled perfectly, and it's remained that way ever since.' But to that natural musicality Bill also brings sense and spontaneity, the products of thorough, rigorous craftsmanship and of an understanding of the human heart that is as deep as it is wide. His is not just the voice beautiful, it is also the voice true; and it is that combination of truth and beauty that makes him arguably the greatest classical actor and speaker of verse in the English theatre today.

Great acting has another component, one that is not so easily defined but one that takes no expert to observe. It is the ability to make an audience *feel*. I don't know what Bill himself feels when he is on stage (some actors internalize their characters' emotions, some do not), but I can testify to his extraordinary ability to tap into the wellsprings of emotion in others.

Last season, in *Long Day's Journey Into Night*, he gave one of his great performances. He played James Tyrone, a popular actor who has squandered his prodigious talents on decades of touring with a melodramatic potboiler. During the long speech in which Tyrone recalls the praise he once received from the great actor Edwin Booth, I began to cry. My assistant director asked me why that particular speech, in a play full of more obviously poignant moments, had moved me so much.

'Bill could have sold out like James Tyrone,' I answered. 'He had great success and every opportunity to leave, but he hadn't sold out, he was here doing exceptional work in these classic plays.' It was so moving to me, that this character Tyrone, who is so tortured by the effects of his greed, was so beautifully played by a man who had given everything for his art.

And because he didn't sell out, the world was favoured with his performances: an astonishing array of them, in roles ranging from Tartuffe to Richard II, from King Lear to Lady Bracknell. Unforgettable performances that made William Hutt that rarity in English Canada: a consummate artist who is also a star.

And, of course, I followed that long-ago inspiration and became an actor myself. Six years after that first momentous visit, I arrived at

Stratford as a young professional to begin rehearsals for my first season. William Hutt came up to me, shook me by the hand and said, 'Welcome home, Richard.' Stratford has been home to me ever since, and the love I have for it will always be bound up with the man who inspired me at the start and whom I am now privileged to call a mentor, a confidant, and a true friend.

'I thank God for you, sir.'*

---

* Quotation from Shakespeare's *Much Ado About Nothing*

DIANA LEBLANC

One of the most acclaimed bilingual actresses in Canada, Diana Leblanc has performed in major theatres across the country, such as The Grand Theatre, Shaw Festival, Tarragon Theatre, Stratford Festival, The Globe Theatre, and Le Théâtre Français. Winner of a Gemini Award for Best Performance on television (La Maison Suspendue), *Ms. Leblanc is the Artistic Director of Le Théâtre Français in Toronto, and has become a director of note, particularly for her unforgettable production of* Long Day's Journey Into Night, *starring William Hutt, at Stratford last year.*

INSTANCES OF WONDER

1962: Stratford, Summer. The hill behind Stratford Collegiate. A tall handsome man, with brown hair and a honeyed voice, is telling us, the acting students of the National Theatre School, that he has doubts about the validity of such training. As he speaks, there is mischief in the eyes and every amused nuance of the voice carries on the summer breeze, so, if I am piqued, I am also intrigued and charmed. This is Bill Hutt, and that summer he is playing Banquo and Prospero, and, however acquired, his skill is astonishing and his presence rivetting.

1994: Stratford, Spring. A rehearsal hall at the Avon. A tall handsome man, with white hair and a honeyed voice, is rehearsing a scene from *Long Day's Journey Into Night*. I am directing Bill Hutt as James Tyrone. In this scene he is telling his younger son Edmund, played by Tom McCamus, about the great compliment Edwin Booth bestowed on him, James, when he was a young actor of great promise. In that instant Bill relives the utter joy in the remembered praise while revealing the great wound carried on a spirit haunted by unfulfilled promise. It is all there. It is a moment beyond skill. It transcends age, time, space, and it leaves me breathless - as it will many who see the production that summer. When

Bill and Martha Henry, playing Mary Tyrone, walk on at the top of Act 1, and we hear their sons, Edmund and Jamie (Tom McCamus and Peter Donaldson), laughing off-stage, I know why I do theatre and I wonder how I got so lucky as to be here.

In the years between 1962 and 1994, I worked with Bill only a few times. Each occasion was significant for me. Bill was theChorus in *Henry V* when I first played at Stratford as Katharine in Michael Langham's bilingual production, which included Douglas Rain, Jean Gascon, Jean-Louis Roux, and Denise Pelletier. 'O, for a muse of fire' indeed. As Ghislaine in *Waltz of the Toreadors* at the Shaw Festival, my heart leapt with anticipation as Bill, playing General de Saint-Pé, greeted me, his long lost love, or so I thought. The antic joy which immediately covered his shock caught my breath every time. When as a novice director I did *The Road to Mecca* at The Grand with Susan Coyne, Frances Hyland, and Bill as Pastor Marius Byleveld, Bill's unfailing courtesy and clear-headed approach to the work were a godsend, and his performance a pleasure to behold as he created a complex character, rigid and sensitive, benign and fearsome.

In 1989 Robin Phillips led the Young Company at the Third Stage. He directed Bill as King Lear, surrounded by a company which included Susan Coyne, Peter Donaldson, Stuart Hughes, John Ormerod, Nancy Palk, Albert Schultz, and Bill Webster. Robin fused Bill's remarkably honed talents and the company's youthful energy into a production as plangent and rapturous as the Elgar music he used so brilliantly. I will never forget Bill's performance. I watched them all spring and summer and could not really say how Robin, Bill, and company achieved their magic, but they did, and I was there. I knew last summer doing *Journey* at the Tom Patterson that I had dared take it on largely because of that summer.

What I don't understand, though, is how Bill as Argan, in Molière's *The Imaginary Invalid* directed by Albert Millaire at the Mainstage, convinced me he was speaking French. Molière, a greatactor himself, who died two hours after playing Argan in 1710, must be smiling. Bill Hutt, a great actor - yes; a unique, irreplaceable actor - yes; but a bilingual one? *Mais oui, vraiment.*

ROBERT C. RAGSDALE

Six years after beginning his career in commercial photography, Robert Ragsdale opened his own studio in Toronto in 1955, specializing in corporate publicity, V.I.P. portraiture, and theatre photography. His early theatre photography consisted mainly of feature photo stories for Toronto Star Weekly *and* Time *magazine, which took him to Broadway many times and across Canada. Having served as official photographer for such companies as the Shaw Festival, Stratford Festival, Canadian Opera Company, Grand Theatre, Young People's Theatre, Theatre Aquarius, the Citadel, et cetera, Mr. Ragsdale has in the course of his distinguished career captured many of the world's leading performers on film, among them Sir Peter Ustinov, William Hutt, Dame Maggie Smith, Martha Henry, Jessica Tandy, Charles Laughton, Christopher Plummer, Glenda Jackson, Harry Belafonte, and Joel Grey. More recently, he has done the production photography for* Aspects of Love *and* The Phantom of the Opera. *A Master of Photographic Arts, a Fellow in the Royal Photographic Society of Great Britain, and the winner of two medals in the International Competition of Theatrical Art held in Yugoslavia, he is also the recipient of the Queen's Silver Jubilee Medal. His photographs have been exhibited in many notable galleries, among them Canada House in London, England; the National Arts Centre in Ottawa; and the National Archives in Ottawa.*

PHOTOGRAPHING WILLIAM HUTT

One of my earliest recollections of William Hutt was photographing him in a scene from *Edward II* for *Time* magazine. He was sandwiched between mattresses by two assassins and dispatched with a red-hot poker thrust into a rather sensitive area where the sun doesn't shine. It's a pity the camera couldn't have recorded the sound emitted by Bill. It was memorable.

Over the years we have collaborated on many photographs - everything from a doddering King Lear and a haughty and disdainful Lady Bracknell in *The Importance of Being Earnest* to an eight-year-old child in The Grand Theatre's production of *The Dining Room*.

To say that he is an extremely versatile actor would be an understatement. However, he does present some problems to a portraitist. Not having the strong aquiline features of a Basil Rathbone, but rather the softer, more rounded features of a Charles Laughton, he makes a photographer rely on the twinkle in the eye, the very malleable and expressive face, and his sense of humour - all of which combine to make photographing him a real joy.

William Hutt
Masks and Faces

Photo Section

ROBERT C. RAGSDALE *f.r.p.s.*

King Lear (1972). *(photo: Robert C. Ragsdale, F.R.P.S. Courtesy of the Stratford Festival Archives)*

ROBERT C. RAGSDALE *f.r.p.s.*

Lady Bracknell in *The Importance of Being Earnest* (1975). *(photo: Robert C. Ragsdale, F.R.P.S. Courtesy of the Stratford Festival Archives)*

ROBERT C. RAGSDALE *f.r.p.s.*

Titus Andronicus (1978). *(photo: Robert C. Ragsdale, F.R.P.S. Courtesy of the Stratford Festival Archives)*

ROBERT C. RAGSDALE *f.r.p.s.*

Sir John Falstaff in *The Merry Wives of Windsor* (1978). *(photo: Robert C. Ragsdale, F.R.P.S. Courtesy of the Stratford Festival Archives)*

ROBERT C. RAGSDALE *f.r.p.s.*

The Fool in King Lear (1980).
(photo: Robert C. Ragsdale,
F.R.P.S. Courtesy of the Stratford
Festival Archives)

ROBERT C. RAGSDALE *f.r.p.s.*

Cardinal Wolsey in *Henry VIII* (1986). *(photo: Robert C. Ragsdale, F.R.P.S. Courtesy of the Stratford Festival Archives)*

ROBERT C. RAGSDALE *f.r.p.s.*

Sir Thomas More in *A Man For All Seasons* (1986). *(photo: Robert C. Ragsdale, F.R.P.S. Courtesy of the Stratford Festival Archives)*

ROBERT C. RAGSDALE *f.r.p.s.*

The Dining Room (1992). *(photo:*
Robert C. Ragsdale, F.R.P.S.
Courtesy of the photographer)

ROBERT C. RAGSDALE *f.r.p.s.*

Ebenezer Scrooge in *A Christmas Carol* (1993). *(photo: Robert C. Ragsdale, F.R.P.S. Courtesy of The Grand Theatre)*

ROBERT C. RAGSDALE *f.r.p.s.*

Harry Raymond in *The Still-born Lover* (1993). *(photo: Robert C. Ragsdale, F.R.P.S. Courtesy of The Grand Theatre)*

PETER SMITH

Above: Scene from *As You Like It* (1959), with (centre) Kate Reid as Celia; Irene Worth as Rosalind; William Hutt as Jaques. *(photo: Peter Smith. Courtesy of the Stratford Festival Archives)*

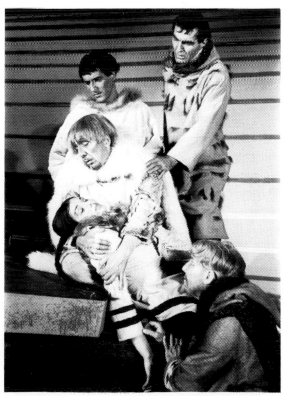

Right: Scene from the Canadian Players' *King Lear* (1961-62), with (L-R) Judith Coates as Cordelia; William Hutt as King Lear; David Renton as Edgar; Kenneth Pogue as Albany and Mervyn Blake as Kent. (photo: Lutz Dille. Courtesy of The Metropolitan Toronto Library Theatre Archives)

LUTZ DILLE

PETER SMITH

Scene from *Troilus and Cressida* (1963), with William Hutt as Pandarus and Peter Donat as Troilus. *(photo: Peter Smith. Courtesy of the Stratford Festival Archives)*

Below: Scene from *Falstaff (Henry IV, Part Two)* (1965), with (L-R) Tony van Bridge as Falstaff; Mervyn Blake as Silence; and William Hutt as Shallow. *(photo: Peter Smith. Courtesy of the Stratford Festival Archives)*

PETER SMITH

Above: Scene from *Uncle Vanya* (1978), with (L-R) Mervyn Blake as Waffles; Brian Bedford as Dr. Astrov; Marti Maraden as Sonya; and William Hutt as Vanya. *(photo: Robert C. Ragsdale, F.R.P.S. Courtesy of the Stratford Festival Archives)*

Left: Scene from The Grand Theatre production of *The Doctor's Dilemma* (1983), with (L-R) Leo Leyden (Sir Patrick Cullen); William Hutt (Sir Ralph Bloomfield Bonington); Gary Reinecke (Sir Colenso Ridgeon); and Barry MacGregor (Mr. Cutler Walpole). *(photo: Robert C. Ragsdale, F.R.P.S. Courtesy of the photographer)*

ROBERT C. RAGSDALE *f.r.p.s.*

Scene from *The Dining Room* (1992), with (L-R) Peter Hutt, Jan Alexandra Smith, Brigitte Robinson, Jonathan Whittaker, William Hutt, and Patricia Collins. *(photo: Robert C. Ragsdale, F.R.P.S. Courtesy of The Grand Theatre)*

Below: Scene from The Grand Theatre production of *The Dining Room* (1992), with William Hutt and Patricia Collins. *(photo: Robert C. Ragsdale, F.R.P.S. Courtesy of the photographer)*

ROBERT C. RAGSDALE *f.r.p.s.*

ROBERT C. RAGSDALE *f.r.p.s.*

Above: William Hutt (Andrew Makepeace Ladd III) and Patricia Collins (Melissa Gardner) in *Love Letters* (1993). *(photo: Robert C. Ragsdale, F.R.P.S. Courtesy of The Grand Theatre)*

MARK SHAWN

Left: Scene from the Mark Shawn Players' production of *Theatre* (1948), with (L-R) Sylvia Shawn, William Hutt (Michael Gosselyn). *(photo: Mark Shawn. Courtesy of Sylvia Shawn)*

William Hutt as Brutus in *Julius Caesar* (1965). *(photo: Peter Smith. Courtesy of the Stratford Festival Archives)*

PETER SMITH

MICHAEL COOPER

Scene from *The School For Scandal* (1987), with (L-R) Faye Cohen as Maid; Sheila McCarthy as Lady Teazle; William Hutt as Sir Peter Teazle; Calla Krause as Maid; and Gerard Theoret as Servant. *(photo: Michael Cooper. Courtesy of the Stratford Festival Archives)*

Scene from *King Lear* (1988), with (L-R) Vincent Dale as Albany; Johnny Lee Davenport as the King of France; John Ormerod as the Fool; William Hutt as King Lear; Jeffrey Hutchinson as Soldier; William Webster as Gloucester; Albert Schultz as Edgar; Susan Coyne as Regan; Peter Donaldson as Kent; Doug Hughes as Burgundy; and Marion Adler as Goneril. *(photo: Michael Cooper. Courtesy of the Stratford Festival Archives)*

PETER SMITH

Richard II (1964). (photo: Peter Smith. Courtesy of the Stratford Festival Archives)

PETER SMITH

Don Adriano de Armado in
Love's Labour's Lost (1964).
*(photo: Peter Smith. Courtesy of
the Stratford Festival Archives)*

PETER SMITH

Gaev in *The Cherry Orchard* (1965). *(photo: Peter Smith. Courtesy of the Stratford Festival Archives)*

DOUGLAS SPILLANE

Khlestakov in *The Government Inspector* (1967). *(photo: Douglas Spillane. Courtesy of the Stratford Festival Archives)*

DOUGLAS SPILLANE

Enobarbus in *Antony and Cleopatra* (1967). *(photo: Douglas Spillane. Courtesy of the Stratford Festival Archives)*

DOUGLAS SPILLANE

Tartuffe (1968). *(photo: Douglas Spillane. Courtesy of the Stratford Festival Archives)*

DOUGLAS SPILLANE

Volpone (1971). *(photo: Douglas Spillane. Courtesy of the Stratford Festival Archives)*

DAVID COOPER

Sir William Gower in *Trelawny of the 'Wells'* (1990). *(photo: David Cooper. Courtesy of The Shaw Festival)*

Argan in *The Imaginary Invalid* (1993). *(photo: Cylla von Tiedemann. Courtesy of the Stratford Festival Archives)*

CYLLA VON TIEDEMANN

James Tyrone in *Long Day's Journey Into Night* (1994). *(photo:
Cylla von Tiedemann. Courtesy of
the Stratford Festival Archives)*

PAMELA BROOK

Born in London, Ontario, Pamela Brook studied in Toronto at Hart House and the Royal Conservatory, apprenticed with the MTC and the Shaw Festival, and toured with Regina's Globe Theatre. She graduated with a M.F.A. from the University of Minnesota, and joined the Stratford Festival in 1970, taking over the role of Maria in The School for Scandal *for the last three weeks of the Spring Tour. She appeared opposite William Hutt in* Tartuffe *at the National Arts Centre, Ottawa, and in the Australian tour of* The Imaginary Invalid. *She was also directed by Hutt at Stratford in* As You Like It *and* Much Ado About Nothing.

SERIOUS FUN

I think of Bill with enormous love. I knew him first through my parents (Mr. and Mrs. John F. Brook) and their association with the Dominion Drama Festival. I was taken in the first and early years of Stratford to see the plays, and as a young girl I dreamt of being there. I met Bill in my own right when I was at Trinity College, University of Toronto, living at St. Hilda's. Bill arrived at Hart House in the late fall of 1966 to direct *Ondine* in which I was playing the title role.

We met in what must have been Robert Gill's small office. I don't remember the audition as being long or complicated. We talked and I read a little of Ondine. That was that. I think at the time I *was* an Ondine, and Bill must have known that he could capitalize on my instincts and theatrical innocence, and protect them. He had my blonde hair cut very short but swept up and out in the back, as if the wind and water were in her hair. I think now that in the weeks of rehearsal he must have instilled his enormous magic and love, tenderness and romance.

I was too young to have acquired strong technical skills. I suspect Bill crafted and constructed a performance around my innocence without my knowing it. Specifically, he would show me technically how I would kiss Hans, standing on my toes, my hands at my sides, winged slightly back. The kiss very simple and not long. A first and original kiss. I remember him standing on the stage demonstrating how the simple kiss would look more passionate than a clichéd, elaborate one. He devised my first entrance with my running at top speed on my toes from the wings stage left, past the house window, and coming to a dead stop (still on my toes) where the centre door had magically blown open. The entrance continued from there to down right, the walk or run always on the front of the foot and lifting up and often ending on the toes - rather like figure skating on the wind or water.

After Ondine was captured in the last act, I remember Bill blocking me in my fishnet on a rock form way down right, and specifically placing my hands, my feet, and the angle of my body to best convey the sadness of her plight. And always making beautiful pictures. I remember in the final parting scene with Hans at a fountain, centre, Bill's blocking me for the last kiss with my arms thrown out behind me, rather like women did before being beheaded, but creating the effect of a Yeatsian swan. And in an earlier love scene with Hans, Bill had me lying on a table having exactly positioned my head and body and arms.

. . .

When I was at St. Hilda's, I used to watch from the upper windows as Robert Gill, with whom I studied, walked down the avenue towards Hart House. He moved as if he were a great pillar on a float. And Bill has always seeemed like that to me.

Sometime during the run of Ondine, Bill told me that someone very special had been in the audience and that this person had enjoyed my performance very much and would be happy to help me, if he could. It was Dr. Guthrie, and in the years following, he did indeed help.

. . .

Dr. Guthrie was no longer alive when I got to Stratford. Bill and Jean Gascon in my years there (1970-74) treated me as a daughter in a theatrical family. In the years since, I've often heard artistic directors use the word 'family' loosely, but with Jean and Bill the word had true meaning. They offered me protection and safety, time to be nurtured and trained.

My first parts there with Bill as a director were Hero in *Much Ado About Nothing* and Celia in *As You Like It*. In teaching us to use the theatre - the centre pillar, the diagonals - Bill would talk about 'thinking up' to the house, in *As You Like It* about 'not speaking unless it improved on silence, not moving unless it improved on stillness.' In *Tartuffe*, in which I replaced as Marianne for the National Arts Centre run, I remember Bill as Tartuffe holding his script out several feet from his body, ensuring sufficient space around him for the command he needed. Now I often think of him doing that when people are madly crowding - doing 'television blocking' - not allowing enough space for the words to travel over some arc.

By the time I played Celia with Bill as Volpone, I was a little older, and it was great fun to begin to be treated by him as a 'woman' on the stage. The Australian tour of *The Imaginary Invalid* was governed by Bill's leadership - but mostly by his enormous sense of fun. It was said that Dr. Guthrie referred to the work as 'serious fun,' and Bill's productions were always that.

MERVYN BLAKE

ACTING FOR HUTT

I think he wasn't in his stride at the time of *Saint Joan* in 1975. It didn't go over very well for some extraordinary reason that I don't know. Bill thought the reviewers hadn't got the heart of the matter. He had a couple of people who were temperamental while wanting to do a good job. The thing about Bill is that sometimes he gets an idea of how he wants to interpret something, and he finds it difficult to change his conception. Also, Bill is usually inclined to think of himself as an intellectual, but in fact he's got an enormous amount of feeling which he doesn't allow to come too much to the fore. But he's extremely good working with actors and very patient.

He gave very perceptive notes and sometimes showed you what to do. I don't mind people showing me what to do. I'm a much better copier than I am an imaginer. He was always kind to me in rehearsal, though I think I gave one of the worst performances I ever gave when directed by him. I'd played the part of Cauchon before, yet I was extremely bad in it for Bill. At one point in rehearsals, after he had worked out the blocking for me and Leslie Yeo (Warwick), we got it just right. And he said to the rest of the company, '*This* is what I want. *This* is how I want it played.' That spoiled it! We never could do it again. Never worked somehow. Leslie was good, but I was awful.

I preferred being in his *Much Ado About Nothing* (1971). It was an easier play, and he's got a very good sense of comedy. We did it in Edwardian period, which Bill likes very much. And he definitely stressed the romantic element. That's what it's all about. Two people who are diametrically opposed to each other, but whose passion finally gets the better of them and they can't help it. I thought Ken Welsh and Jane Casson did very well as Benedick and Beatrice. I mean they were not ideally cast, but they did extremely well. And Leon Pownall, who was wonderfully good-looking then -young and slim - played Claudio.

Bill gave me a lot of latitude as Dogberry. I wasn't able to perfect the role early on, but I was able to over the season. He gave me a rough idea of Dogberry, but didn't *push* me to any length. I was inclined to overact it, to start with. Dogberry *is* a comic character, but I learned in my experience that a comic character isn't comic because you've tried to make him comic. He's comic because he is himself that kind of person.

I enjoyed making-up for that character. Olivier gave me a good tip once. I asked, 'How do you develop your characters, Larry?' He replied, 'I like to go around on the tube [the underground], watching people's faces. Sometimes a nose or someone's squint will give me an idea of what the character should be. I don't build from the inside. I build from the outside.' I'm inclined to do that, and although he wouldn't say it himself, Bill is also more external. I'm not as polished as Bill is, but I like getting comic characters because they're fun to do.

BARBARA BUDD

Barbara Budd is the co-host of the CBC radio flagship show As It Happens. *She spent five seasons as an actress with the Stratford Festival from 1975-1980. She has been heard in over a hundred radio dramas and is a frequent guest with* The Royal Canadian Air Farce. *Her recordings include three Juno award-winning albums on the Classical Kids Label. Miss Budd was born in St. Catharines, Ontario, one year in the 1950s.*

THE OLD FANTASTICAL DUKE OF DARK CORNERS

I'll wager that most people envision William Hutt bathed in light. But most of my brightest memories of him - he's in the dark.

As a kid I was afraid of the dark. You just can't be sure of anything when you can't see clearly. The unknown looms larger than life, and things are rarely what they appear.

I met William Hutt in the dark.

It was in 1974 when I auditioned for the Stratford Festival Company. I was summoned into the Avon Theatre from a hot, sun-lit lobby. I was already nervous and as my eyes adjusted to the sudden 'non-light' I could only just make out the two figures. Bill was assisting the new Artistic Director, Robin Phillips, with the auditions, as he too would be directing in the up-coming season. There the two of them sat at a table - a gooseneck lamp dimly illuminating a tiny island in that sea of black. Beyond them - a brightly lit stage. The warmth and brightness of that stage seemed miles away from me.

I remember sitting there not knowing what to expect and bewildered by some of their questions. Actually, it was Robin who asked most of them. It just wasn't the sort of interview I had anticipated. After an unthreatening little chat about my theatre school training and the train ride from Toronto, came the toughies.

It went something like this:

Robin: Can you ride a unicycle?

Me: No.

Robin: Can you juggle?

Me: No.

Robin: Can you walk a tight-rope?

Me: No.

Robin: Can you tap-dance?

Me: No.

Robin: Can you do a handstand?

Me: No.

Robin: A headstand?

Me: Not unless I'm up against a wall...which I may be now.

Robin: How about a cartwheel?

Me: No.

Robin: Can you rollerskate?

Me: No. This is going awfully well, don't you think?

Oh brother! I was batting zero. I was feeling completely defeated, but trying to keep a brave face under their scrutiny. Just as the gulf between that dimly-lit island and the shores of that great, bright stage had widened to an impossible distance, Bill stepped in. He was staring down at a plucky, though none-the-less, sinking Canadian kid, and he threw me a truly Canadian life-line. With a rather meaningful look, and I should add, a great deal of warmth, he asked:

'Can you ice-skate?'

Now, truth be told, I spend most of my time on the ice, flat on my back...but how were they ever going to know? I didn't see how they could ask me to demonstrate my skill, or lack of it, any time soon. It was August, thank God. So, I figured, oh, what the hell....

'Yes. Yes, I can.' I nearly wept my answer. But then, overcome by candour, I added: 'But I'm not exactly Barbara Ann Scott.'

'Never mind, dear,' cooed Bill. 'Neither is Barbara Ann Scott...anymore.'

Bill has a tremendous sense of fun, and a pretty darn good dash of devilry too. Over twenty years, I've seen the old Nick in his eyes many a time. Because of that, it was hard to be intimidated by him again. I have real respect for him and his talent, but after that first meeting, I never feared him again.

When rehearsals began for the next season, I was there. I wondered if he would remember me. Robin and Bill had crossed the country and had auditioned hundreds of actors, so it wouldn't have surprised me if six months later we would need to be re-introduced.

My first 'call' as a member of the company was for the main stage production of Shaw's *Saint Joan*. Bill was the director. In the line-up for coffee in the Green Room prior to the first rehearsal, I found myself by chance behind him. While mustering the nerve to say hello, and wondering whether he would remember me, he turned to me and said:

'Well, if it isn't Barbara Ann Scott...and it isn't!'

Bill can always make me laugh and I think he probably got a kick out of the fact too that he didn't intimidate me. I know that many young actors were so much in awe of him, that it took them ages before they could call him by his first name. Frankly, I think he liked being called 'Mr. Hutt.' But I remember going up to him, one day soon after rehearsals began, and rather boldly saying 'I hope you don't mind, but I don't think I want to call you "Mr. Hutt" anymore. Can I call you Bill, and I'll just "think" the Mr. Hutt bit?' I can remember his response exactly, and it was wonderfully funny but unsuitable for print - so I'll just leave it at that, and say that from then on, I called him 'Bill.'

In subsequent years as I got to know him better, it became a sort of habit of mine to go around to his dressing room for a visit. While he was putting his make-up on, we would exchange jokes. This was not a nightly habit by any means, but just when I heard one, or remembered one that I thought he might get a charge out of. Sometimes I just went 'round because I wanted a 'Hutt Hit.'

In the early years at Stratford, I shared a dressing room with three other actresses. One night, we were rather shocked that Bill knocked at our door, about thirty minutes before the show. He wasn't prone to visiting other rooms. He summoned me to his dressing room for a chat. My room-mates figured I was in 'deep' for something, but it turned out Bill had a joke for me, and I hadn't popped in for a while.

He wasn't beyond trying to break me up on stage either. In the 1976 production of *The Tempest*, in which he was a deeply moving Prospero, I was one of fifteen actors cast as 'Sprites of the Island.' We were like a chorus, silently under-scoring the spells cast by Shakespeare's magician. The idea was that we would remain stock-still until specific cues, when we would move in slow motion and in perfect unison. The choreography was set, and we were directed to even breathe in unison. It took a great deal of concentration on the sprites' part. I have no idea how impressive it looked to an audience. I just know that it was not one of my most cherished roles on any stage, anytime, and Bill knew this.

We were performing on the proscenium arch stage of the Avon Theatre. At one point in the production, the sprites were on stage, but Prospero was not. Bill would stand in the wings, waiting for his next entrance. But before he moved into his downstage position, he would just 'stop off' for a little moment at the upstage entrance. I was on stage concentrating like mad on 'superb spriting' just about two feet away from that entrance. And from the dark offstage, I would hear his voice. He would tell me jokes and what he had for dinner. He would ask me ludicrous questions. He didn't go so far as to give me an obscene phone-call in person...but he came pretty darn close. He could be outrageous. But he always gave himself enough time to move quietly downstage into position, to enter once again as Prospero, and be absolutely compelling and magical.

We took *The Tempest* on tour and one of our stops was The Grand Theatre in Kingston. One night, about forty-five minutes from the end of the show, a fire broke out in the theatre. (The sprites had nothing to do with it. We were upstairs in our dressing rooms, probably playing 'Scrabble.')

I don't know what it is about people in a theatre when alarms go off. Perhaps it is the darkness that enshrouds them but you can hear the reaction sweep through, and there are always the few that experience real panic. Obviously, that's the worst thing in a situation like that. The cast members not on stage at the time were pretty calm, but not sure what to do...all that 'show must go on' stuff. Then the stage manager's voice announced that the theatre should be cleared and the audience was asked to leave calmly. We grabbed our coats and make-up kits, as the alarms continued alarming, and headed downstairs to the stage door to go out into the February night. We had heard the announcement to the audience and figured the house had been cleared, so what we saw was pretty surprising as we passed the stage. There was Bill sitting on the apron of the stage, his sandalled feet dangling over the edge, and fifty or so rapt audience members still sitting in their seats giving him their undivided attention. He was telling them in his own words how the play ends. These stalwarts who sat on, as the fire department swept in, got a rare performance.

When I think of all the faces of William Hutt, it's logical that the images of Lady Bracknell, Prospero, the Duke in *Measure for Measure*, and Timon of Athens come to mind. But after Lady Bracknell, my favourite memory of the actor is as James Tyrone.

At the time of writing, Bill is starring in his third production of *Long Day's Journey Into Night*, this time with the remarkable Martha Henry. But in 1977 Bill played James Tyrone for the first time at The Grand Theatre in London. Robin Phillips directed the production that starred Bill and Jessica Tandy, with the late Graeme Campbell as Jamie, and Bill's nephew Peter Hutt as Edmund. I played Cathleen, the Irish maid. It was a special experience for several reasons. We were five actors, working with a beloved director on a beautifully written piece of theatre. And we all grew closer, as we endured a ferocious South Western Ontario winter together...away from our own homes...away from our own families.

Though we all had apartments while rehearsing in London, Bill and Robin and I had homes in Stratford too. On our day off each week, we would go home. One night there was a truly terrible storm. Bill really wanted to make the forty mile trip back to Stratford. Robin didn't think it was wise, given the conditions, but he said he also didn't want to see anyone make the drive alone. We decided to all go in Bill's Cadillac. If we were going to be buried in a drift, we could do it together.

One can't describe the road from London to Stratford to anyone who hasn't driven it in a blizzard. It is treacherous. The frequent white-outs are sudden, disorienting, and terrifying. This was just such a storm. With over a foot of new snow, and even more in the forecast, it was probably mad to attempt it...but we were determined.

As we sat waiting in the parking lot for the car to warm up and the windows to defrost, Bill turned to Robin in the front seat and me in the back. 'Okay, let's make a pact right here. If for any reason any one of us wants to turn back - we will. Okay?' We agreed and off we set.

It was one of the most nerve-wracking rides I can remember. At times we would have to come to a complete stop in the darkness to find where the road was. The white-outs were that blinding. Robin navigated, as Bill sometimes couldn't see the side of the two-lane highway. Sometimes we would come out of a white-out to find that we were driving on the wrong side of the road. Fortunately, there was no other traffic to speak of. After counting ten or more cars abandoned in drifts that nearly buried them, it seemed best to stop keeping a tally.

We didn't speak much. We were far too tense. No one mentioned turning back, though. After we had been travelling for almost an hour at a snail-like speed, Bill broke the silence that had fallen. 'Barbara,' he said, 'I'm going to tell you a story.' And he started to speak in a quiet, slow, and deliberate voice. He spoke of a man lost in a foreign country - not knowing which direction to go, what road to take. I got totally caught up in the story. I think we all did, even Bill. So that it wasn't until almost the end, that I realized I'd heard this story before - but not like this. It wasn't a story at all. It was a riddle I had been told years before. Bill laid it out like a mystery and when he posed the riddle at the end, our guesses took us the rest of the way home. I don't know to this day if Robin already knew the answer, but if he did, he didn't let on either. When I think back on it now, I have to admire the concentration it took to drive us through that storm, and the art with which he wove that riddle into a story at the same time, so beautifully.

There are some actors who are slightly embarrassed by their fame. They don dark glasses, and shuffle head-bowed, hoping no one will recognize them on the street. They just want to blend into the crowd when they leave the theatre. I don't think Bill is one of those actors. Or maybe he found out a long time ago that anonymity wasn't possible for him. He is a rather imposing figure, and he lives in a rather small town, where the theatre is the major industry. So the 'sightings' of Mr. Hutt are frequent. He does, after all, have to push a shopping cart around the grocery store, and have his tires checked, and buy flowers for his garden - like anyone else. But Bill has a way about him. And when you catch him being 'him,' you are always a little surprised, and more than a little delighted.

At our family cottage in Muskoka, there is a giant blue heron...a magnificent bird with a tremendous wing span...breathtaking when it takes flight...and utterly majestic when it comes to light on the end of our dock. It stands over three feet tall. Sometimes it will just pose in perfect stillness for as long as ten minutes at a time. Then suddenly, it sweeps off, with a great show. It flies into our bay in the early morning usually. But one night, I was out studying the night sky, and I heard a splashing on the beach in front of me. For a moment I was frightened, wondering what large animal was so near to me in the blackness. As my eyes became accustomed to the dark, I saw it was the heron strolling casually in the shallow water.

Bill is a bit like that heron. You know that there have to be others...but not many.

PATRICIA HAMILTON

Patricia Hamilton (b. 1937) has a B.F.A. (Carnegie Tech, 1960) and years of training and experience in the United States, England, and Canada. She founded the Master Class programme in Toronto for professional actors, winning the Brenda Donohue Award (1987) for significant contribution to Toronto's theatre community. With a Genie (A Bird in the House), *a Gemini* (The Road to Avonlea), *and a Dora* (I Am Yours) *to her credit as actress, she continues her commitment to Canadian theatre as Director of the Advanced Actors' Workshop at the Banff Centre for the Arts.*

MASTER DIRECTOR

(The following is extracted from an edited version of Keith Garebian's interview with Patricia Hamilton in Toronto, April 6, 1994.)

I've known him as an actor for as long as Stratford has existed. As a teenager, I went to the very first season, so I've seen his work for many, many years and admired it enormously. He is our premier classical actor in terms of his use of the verse. My admiration for him stems from many different points of view in acting, but mainly the first thing I would have to say is the way he deals with the text. His clarity, his simplicity, his Canadianism - those were the things that really attracted me.

We have always in this country felt like the poor sister of England - particularly where their greatest playwright is concerned. It's a natural enough thing to feel because, indeed, they do Shakespeare extremely well, and we've always admired that. However, I think Robin Phillips has done us a great service by saying that we must do Shakespeare in our own voice. Bill Hutt has been doing that from the very beginning, and I think that *that* appealed to me more than anything else because what I'm trying to do at Banff with the Advanced Actors' Workshop programme is develop Canadian actors. I have a great interest in directors from other countries bringing their skills and wisdom to give to us, without changing the way we express ourselves. So, if we were going to do Shakespeare, I was very concerned that it should be Canadian Shakespeare. And that was the principal reason why I approached Bill. He is the man who really commands that Stratford stage. There is never any effort behind his getting to every seat in that house. That's vocal, but it's not simply vocal. That's an *understanding* of the stage, that's an *understanding* of the audience, that's an *ease* with the text, that's years and years and years of experience. There is no attempt to do the text with an English accent, and he makes it clear that that isn't necessary in order to bring out the music.

Basically, we have a neutral speech, and Bill Hutt has a poetic ear, so he can use his own speech to express the words of Shakespeare. There's something emotional to hearing Shakespeare done in your own accent. It takes away some of the barrier between audience and actor. It makes the identification more immediate. It's important that we do it that way, and I think it's perfectly accepted now all across the country. I think you'd be hard pressed to find people doing British accents in Shakespeare in this country any more, and that's directly attributable to Bill and to Robin.

As an actor, Bill is *par excellence*, but it was not as an actor that I was interested in Mr. Hutt in the fall of '92. It was because of clarity - not just of speech, but of thinking. Every performance of Bill's that I had seen had a clear through-line - no matter who was directing him. He knew where the character was going, he knew what the character had to accomplish, he knew where the character sat in the play. So although I had never seen him as a director, I assumed that he had some overall vision of the play, as well as an actor's interior vision.

The Advanced Actors' Workshop at the Banff Centre is a programme devoted to advanced actors - actors who have been out in the profession for at least five years, sometimes they've been out there for fifteen or twenty - who want to go back and do some more training. We wanted to be able to say to actors: 'We'd like you to take more chances. We'd like you to dig deeper. It doesn't matter what the result is. We're not result-oriented here. We're not trying to sell this to the public. We're trying to upgrade your skills.' I don't know if there's any other place in the country where that kind of training is offered to actors, where they can step away from the demands of the market place, get a stipend that is enough to keep the wolf from the door and go back and investigate the roots of their interest in theatre.

We found that actors were very interested in this idea, in stepping away from the market place itself and doing some work that was art for art's sake, if you will, where the process was more important than the product, where they could, indeed, spend the time working on blocks or problems or difficulties that actors have. So, in order to do that, we conceived of a three-year plan. Each summer I would provide them with a different director, with a different particular task, and, as originally conceived, we were going to do a very heavily text-based work of some kind the first summer - Shakespeare, probably.

I talked to Martha Henry and said, 'Do you think Bill Hutt would consider directing for us under these conditions? It's not a pressure situation, and I am not interested in the final product as much as I am interested in the six weeks of rehearsal.' And she said, 'Well, you can only ask him, but I certainly think he might be interested.' So I approached him and when I put the proposition to him, he said that he was very interested and would I put that in writing, please, and he would respond. I did that and sent him some material about the project, and he responded favourably.

Now I don't think the three-year plan ever meant very much to Bill. I don't think he believed, first of all, that actors would stay with you for three years. I don't think he had much sympathy for the ideas behind it. He never said anything negative about it, but I just got the idea from him that he was interested in choosing people to do *Twelfth Night* because that was the project he came up with very quickly when he knew the number of people I had. We had done nothing but tragedy, and I was very happy that we were going to do *Twelfth Night*, and he wanted to do the best production of *Twelfth Night* possible. But I had to keep telling him that we were not just choosing people for *Twelfth Night*; we were choosing people for three years.

I do a cross-Canada audition tour every year, usually with the director, and we see upwards of four to five hundred people. We go from Vancouver to Halifax. I knew that Bill wasn't up to that kind of trip. Not only that, I didn't want to choose people for three years with only Bill, the first-year director. I wanted to have all three directors with me, and clearly I wasn't going to be able to do that. Bill goes to Florida in January, and that's when we usually do the tour, so we came up with the solution that I would do the initial tour. Then we would have call-backs in Toronto. I tried to choose people from a number of perspectives. First of all, I tried to choose people who would be correct for the roles in *Twelfth Night* because, indeed, you do have to think about that. I didn't know what the second year's play was going to be at that point because we were up in the air after we lost Robert Lepage to Europe. (Robert and Tomson Highway were supposed to create a new piece for the second year.) But I also chose people who were interested in the three-year plan, who were interested in the ensemble, who might at the end of three years take this expertise they would get and disseminate it. In other words, I was looking for leaders.

At any rate, I brought about forty people together for Bill to see in call-back situation in Toronto. He saw the forty over two days. He didn't want them to do anything from *Twelfth Night*, so they all did a Shakespearean piece of one kind or another, and he interviewed them. He made extensive notes, and then we had a couple of meetings and talked about all of them. He went home to Stratford to think about it. He called me from there and said, 'If you were to choose your twelve, what would they be? I don't guarantee to take them, but I want to know who they are.' So I gave him a list, and he called me back an hour later with his list - which was fairly close to mine. We had a sort of battle about getting a fourth woman into the company of twelve. I was absolutely adamant that we couldn't have a three-year programme with only three women. I suggested a woman for Feste, and he went mad. I thought it was very strange because he had played both Lady Bracknell and one of the Brewster sisters in *Arsenic and Old Lace*. He just thought it was a ludicrous idea and said something which did make me laugh. 'Don't you understand? Feste is the wisdom of the play?' We compromised by having a woman play Fabian, and I got my fourth woman.

In terms of the time we spent in Banff, I think it was excellent. I like to think that we do provide a first-class situation for our directors. We hold them in high regard. We call them Master Directors, and we have them there for the accumulated knowledge that they bring. We value that. I told him: 'I want you to teach them how to speak the verse in a Canadian way. I want you to teach them what you know about verse speaking. That is my *major* interest this summer. The medium for doing this is the production of *Twelfth Night*. But I don't mind if the production is mediocre.' Now, his back went *right up!* There was no way he was going to do a *mediocre production!* And, of course, he didn't. He did the most successful production we've had there to date. It was pretty well sold out the whole time, and it was a production with a really gentle, marvellous tone to it - a dark kind of *Twelfth Night* with a lovely overall directorial vision.

He did a major cutting of the script and said on the first day: 'You're going to have to placate that Ted Atherton person who's playing Feste because I've cut his role to death.' But, indeed, Ted Atherton, as you will see if you read the reviews, was remarkable. And it was from Bill. It's not the way Ted would have chosen to play it on his own. He played it as an old man, and Bill obviously drew on his own two interpretations of that part. He was generous with that, and Ted didn't find it a problem to take the cuts at all. It's such a beautiful play. The atmosphere is so summery. In this case, it was dark, but still the poetry is so beautiful and the story, simple and lovely. The characters are good people. Viola is a truly good human being, and there are no real villains, except Malvolio who is a comic villain and not really a villain at all. Bill worked very hard with Andy Massingham, who was a very young Sir Toby Belch, and with Chris Heyerdahl who played Aguecheek. Andy Massingham's background is physical clowning - a lot of falling down and stuff like that. Well, Bill wanted to work against that, and Andy, who is a very intelligent actor and a very hard worker, found it difficult to go for what Bill wanted, but what he came up with was a sour, alcoholic, bitter man who went after the things he wanted but didn't enjoy them very much. Bill kept saying: 'This is not funny. We don't want to play this for comic buffoonery. This is not Falstaff.' I think Andy did a remarkable job and learned a great deal.

Patrick Clark designed a unit set which was meant to last for the three years. It was a delightful set with a slight rake that brought the thing forward to the audience. It really was basically a rake with a tree and some entrances, exits, and archways. They had more Edwardian costumes in stock than anything else, so they decided to go Edwardian - and that added a nice touch to it. It was fine for Bill because he understood that period very well, and he taught the actors something about how to move in those clothes. The man is a fountain of knowledge about classical theatre. This knowledge isn't going to be with us forever.

And the actors had a wonderful time with Bill. He also passed on lots of wonderful theatre anecdotes. I'll just give you one example. Viola, who was being played by Vickie Papavs, has a line where she has to say something and then she has to hesitate and say something else. He gave her a technical way of doing that. He said, 'Instead of hesitating and then saying the next line, say the first word of the hesitation line and then go on as if you almost know what you're going to say, then think of the rest of it. Do that three times.' She did, and it was absolutely heart-stopping. He said: 'I got that from Guthrie.'

So, there are marvellous little tricks of the trade, but behind them all is a really clear vision of what he wanted to do with *Twelfth Night* and what *Twelfth Night* was. He's done these plays so many times, he knows them so well. I couldn't imagine that these young actors, who are in their early thirties, could sit in a room with him for three hours and not learn something.

He had a bit of a health problem part way through the summer. We were getting close to the tech rehearsals. He was having difficulty breathing and he was waking up with his heart pounding. One night we ended up in hospital. It just seemed unwise to let it go. And while we were in hospital and he was being given various things to test whether his heart was affected - it turned out to be nothing serious, probably the altitude as much as anything else and anxiety - he told me that although he was enjoying the experience very much, he hadn't directed a lot lately and what he felt was that there was a real gap between him and the actors - not a gap of years so much as a gap of experience. He could have stood up and done all those parts. He wasn't quite as confident about how to tell them to do it. He said: 'I know I'm using too many words. I know what I want, but I can't get it across succinctly.' He was having just a little anxiety on the level of his direction. But that's the only hesitation he seemed to have about the work he did.

He responded *extremely* positively to that group. He rented a great big Cadillac - a more unsuitable car for going around the mountains probably doesn't exist - but he rented this Cadillac and he would get one of the boys in the company to drive it for him and on days off he would take them all for outings into the mountains. He was very generous to the company and warm towards them, and they all loved him, I think. They gave him a beautiful briefcase with his initials on it when it was over. He made a lovely speech about how well he felt they had done and how responsive they had been to his direction. And he said: 'I love Stratford. I have been there for many years, but I am not unaware that sometimes at Stratford things are hollow and sound as if it's all sound and fury. And I think that you people have achieved something much greater than that.' And they had - partly because Shakespeare in an intimate space is much easier to play than Shakespeare in that big theatre. But he had also instilled in them the real heart of that play and what it meant.

He really did a lovely job for us, but he also did what I asked him to do - which was to pass on his wisdom about verse-speaking and other things. I think the reason this *Twelfth Night* was so popular was because it was totally accessible. It was clearly spoken. It was one of the clearest productions of Shakespeare I've ever seen. You felt the actors were talking in your living room and talking language that you understood. That's the virtue of this Canadian approach. I heard people saying in the lobby: 'I never knew Shakespeare was so much like us.' A high compliment and what we were really after.

The actors would all tell you now, a year and a half later, that they had a wonderful time. And they did. I think some of them found his directions confusing at times or hard to follow. He had very specific ideas. But that's the normal struggle of a rehearsal process. You have to understand that we're asking actors to do things they've not been asked to do before. That's going to bring up tension in any actor, no matter who the director is. They know that they're having to dig deeper and that makes them edgy and nervous. But, basically, it was a happy summer. I think they will all tell you now that they learned an enormous amount. If they had to say something about Bill's direction, they would call it old-fashioned, probably - not pejoratively. It was just something they weren't used to or something that was harder for them to get their heads around. He knew he was imparting something that would be very valuable to them, and really the value of it has now sunk in for those actors. They know it more now than they did then. Isn't that the way with all really important knowledge? It takes some time to sink in.

*Cast and Credits for *Twelfth Night*
Directed By *William Hutt*
Set and Costumes By *Patrick Clark*
Lighting By *Harry Frehner*
Stage Manager *Winston Morgan*
Assistant Stage Manager *Jeanne LeSage*

Orsino *(John Ralston)*; Valentine *(Ian Robison)*; Curio *(Drew Carnwath)*; Viola *(Vicki Papavs)*; Sebastian *(Andrew Dolha)*; Sea Captain/Priest *(James Kirchner)*: Antonio *(Vieslav Krystyan)*; Olivia *(Sharon Heldt)*; Maria *(Valerie Planche)*; Sir Toby Belch *(Andrew Massingham)*; Sir Andrew Aguecheek *(Chris Heyerdahl)*; Malvolio *(Mark Christmann)*; Fabian *(Carol Dover)*; Feste *(Ted Atherton)*; Maid *(Mieko Ouchi)*

PART THREE: THE MAN

MERVYN BLAKE

POMP AND CIRCUMSTANCE

From my early days at Stratford, after arriving in 1957, I felt that Bill was, to a great degree, over-excitable about things. Despite his stage gifts - height, voice, presence - he used to get over-excited, by which I mean over-exuberant. For instance, he had to go on for a couple of performances as Hamlet when Chris Plummer hurt his ankle. He was very good in the part, having played it earlier on a Canadian Players tour. And when he took the curtain, he used to take it like a ballet star, with elaborate bows. That was pure over-exuberance.

Gradually over the years, he controlled that. And it has been wonderful to see him take control of himself to become poised and the consummate actor he is now. But it's been a long, steady, determined process.

I'll never forget when I was playing Kent to his Lear in 1972, directed by David William. It was the time when Canada was playing hockey against the Soviets. Everyone was watching the game backstage on monitors. Just before the terrific storm scene, he came out and suddenly broke the performance by saying, 'Great news! Great news! We've won!' There was a huge cheer, but Teddy Atienza, who was playing the Fool, was absolutely furious. 'How can I go on as the Fool now in the storm?'

It was one of those things that was completely spontaneous. He couldn't help himself, but *that* he has managed to control now to a huge extent.

That incident stands out because it was against all professionalism. Not that it wasn't sentimentally right, but he should have waited for the interval to utter it, and not done it in the middle of a very crucial moment of the play.

Bill has always been pompous, but that's part of his make-up. He has been able to make his personality assimilate that pomposity, and somehow it's not obnoxious. A wonderful example is when Bill first walks into either the first rehearsal or the first reading. It's always an *occasion* to see him come in. He walks in, waits till everyone looks at him, and then either speaks or doesn't. That's pompous, but it's a natural thing - natural to an actor. He's tall, has a good voice, and when he walks onto the stage, he naturally wants everyone to look at him. You can make fun of it occasionally, but it's quite natural.

At the Church Restaurant dinner in honour of Richard Monette's fiftieth birthday, which was crammed with hundreds of people, Bill wore all his medals and orders. He was the last one to speak and said, 'I've come out in this vulgar display of medals because Richard was born at the time when I was awarded them. And I'm wearing them in honour of him.'

I've seen him be pompous on stage. Because he had back problems when he played Richard II in 1964, he tended to use his affliction to strike Christ-like poses of pain and suffering. That, we used to say, was Bill Hutt at his worst because he was taking advantage of his own pain. That was pomposity in reverse.

The worst thing one's heard is that he allows his pomposity to get the better of him. But I don't agree. I think that what people think is pompous is his being poised and looking over a situation and being in command of it.

On the European tour of *King Lear*, Bill had the talent to lead when required to do so - one of the great things that Bill is absolutely marvellous at. He was a wonderful ambassador for us. He gave some of the most wonderful speeches for us, and everyone took hats off to him. He has the intellect and the ability. A great pity that at one time when he was being considered for the artistic directorship that things weren't settled in the minds of the board members. They didn't know whether the job should go to Bill or Douglas Campbell or someone else. They settled on the dual leadership of Jean Gascon and John Hirsch - which didn't work out.

BARRY MACGREGOR

After beginning his career in 1949 by working in repertory theatre, television, radio, and film in the U.K., Barry MacGregor (b. 1936) acted with the Royal Shakespeare Company from 1961 to 1964. He first appeared at the Stratford Festival, Canada, in 1964, where he has since chalked up fifteen seasons, supporting such performers as Alan Bates, Dame Maggie Smith, William Hutt, and Brian Bedford, playing diverse roles in Shakespeare, Webster, Goldsmith, Wilde, and Molière, and serving as Company Manager. A stint as Artistic Director of the Bastion Theatre in B.C. prepared him for future administrative challenges. In 1981 he became a leading actor and manage-ment associate at the Shaw Festival, where his roles included Higgins (Pygmalion), *Mendoza/Devil* (Man and Superman), *John Tarleton* (Mis-alliance), *and the Inquisitor* (St. Joan). *In addition to his theatre appear-ances across Canada and the U.S., Mr. MacGregor has appeared in the CBC-TV mini-series,* Dieppe, *and can be heard frequently on CBC Radio's* Ideas.

TWO MEMORIES

My first impression of Bill was thirty-one years ago in Stratford during my first visit to North America. I was gazing out of the Green Room window overlooking the car park (this was the original car park) when I observed a white Chevrolet Impala, with red seats, pulling into the stage door area of the parking spaces. The car stopped, and from the driver's seat emerged a tall, elegant man who then walked with a gentle but positive gait towards the stage door. Two things crossed my mind: the car was fantastic; and the person driving it was elegant, strong, and rather daunting, but he suited the car.

In 1966 and 1967 I was lucky enough to become a member of Michael Langham's Festival company during his final two years as Artistic Director. Bill was a leading member of that company, and we have worked together on and off for the last thirty years - at Stratford, at the Grand Theatre in London, Ontario, and at the Shaw Festival. Many memories flood into the video section of my brain - all happy ones - but the following story, which I swear is true, is one I recall with fondness and humour.

The place: The Grand Theatre, Kingston (sister theatre to the Grand in London, Ont.). The date: February, 1976. The performance: Stratford's touring production of *The Tempest*. Bill was Prospero, Nicky Pennell was Ariel, I (the Company Manager) played Trinculo. We were into the second act and only Prospero and Ariel were on stage.

As it was a Robin Phillips production, there was a lot of smoke. But this particular night, the fog/smoke machine, under our false stage, fell over and started to smoulder. As our smoke billowed forth, so did the toxic contents of the fire. The crew realized what was happening, and started to claw their way under the set to retrieve and extinguish the problem. By now the smoke was so thick on stage, no one in the wings could see either Bill or Nicky. Bill somehow sensed that the audience was having a visual problem too, so he moved downstage. Nicky could not see a thing as Bill moved forward, so he quite naturally moved forward too. As matters progressed towards disaster, I turned to Alec Cooper, our chief electrician, and asked: 'Do you want the show stopped?' 'Yes,' came the quick reply. The Stage Manager went onto the stage to advise people that as we were experiencing technical difficulties, we would have to clear the theatre. This announcement came as Bill was in the middle of a long passage. He stopped and met the interruption with total incredulity. Then, as the import of the situation became apparent, he walked forward and gave the audience, who were by now leaving the auditorium, the most wonderful, slow, and graceful bow.

The fire department arrived after the audience had left, and a fireman wearing everything possible arrived backstage, put a large black case and oxygen bottle at my feet and asked how he could get onto the stage. I reported his question to Bill who, without batting an eyelid, said: 'I hope you told him he would have to audition.'

Over the past number of years, I have watched Bill as an actor. The performances - Lady Bracknell, Timon, the Ambassador in *The Stillborn Lover*, et cetera - are so gentle, strong, real, and generous, that it is a joy to be on stage with him, as indeed it is an honour to be in the same profession.

Bill, I salute you and I thank you for many happy, funny, and very real and human moments.

JAMES BLENDICK

HE AND CLASS GO TOGETHER

My wife, Mary, and I have always found it wonderful to spend time with Bill in his own tasteful surroundings. As host, he creates a relaxing atmosphere which allows his guests to feel totally at home. It's inevitable that we all gather in his kitchen while he tends bar - which usually consists of his pouring vintage wine or making his superb martinis. As he serves *hors d'oeuvres*, he gets his guests happily settled so that he can attend to making dinner. It's an evening filled with laughter - and he does love to laugh. Believe it or not, there's very little discussion about the theatre. It's always a five-star evening. Whether in a hotel, a restaurant, or in his own home, he spares no expense. Quite frankly, I don't think I could see him any other way. It seems that he and class go together.

KEITH GAREBIAN

STAR BRIGHT

For his seventy-fourth birthday, I sent him a card expressing the hope that he'd be around for his hundredth, and joked that he was already most of the way there. It is, indeed, difficult not to believe that at his centenary, God willing, he shall be attempting another character role at Stratford- *-One Hundred Years On* at the Tom Patterson, let's say, or *The Importance of Being Cherished* at the Avon, or, perhaps, *Much Ado About Everything* at the Festival stage. Jeremy Brett once remarked of him: 'Caviar to the general. He's not a "one of "; he's unique!'

The awesome chronology at the end of this book is but a summary of what, for most actors, would amount to several distinguished careers rolled into one. At some point in his legendary career, he said to himself that he was going to be one of the best actors this country had produced. He also deliberately set out to win stardom in a country where this was considered to be blushingly immodest. There is Eric House's famous anecdote from the early fifties about Hutt who was then only fourth or fifth fiddle to others at Stratford. Having enjoyed comic success as Froth and Hortensio, Hutt fancied himself rather more importantly than was appropriate to his rank as a company member. While applying make-up in his dressing room, which he shared with five other actors, he remarked: 'One day I'm going to be a star in this theatre, because I'm a good Canadian, a Torontonian.'

'Come on, Bill. That's all crap,' Eric House responded.

'No, no. There's no point in being in this business unless you aim for the top. One day I won't be here unless I'm a star.'

And star he did become, though only after playing a host of supporting character roles that sharpened his talent without necessarily satisfying his ambition or ego. Today, he chuckles at his own impertinence, adding: 'I don't know that I set out so much as to become a star, but I certainly set out to make Herbie Whittaker one day start calling people in this country stars, and I succeeded.' For the most part ... though critic emeritus Whittaker's conservatism still draws his displeasure, especially over *Whittaker's Theatricals* where Sarah Bernhardt, Edmund Kean, Mrs. Patrick Campbell, John Gielgud, and Richard Burton are treated like glorious constellations in the theatrical firmament, but where the only Canadians to be bannered as stars are John Colicos ('The Shooting Star') and Donald Sutherland ('The Ungainly Star'). Hutt has to be satisfied with the modest title 'Our Man of Distinction.' Well, the man of distinction is not so easily appeased.

'I'm a man of distinction because I stayed here? He didn't even call me a star in that, did he?'

And after that acid, a splash of ironic laughter.

He knows his rank and expects deference, even when this leads to comic one-upmanship as at the Church Restaurant one evening many years ago when I took him to dinner. 'I'll go on one condition: that I pay for the drinks.'

Familiar with his preference for cathedral-size martinis, I was only too happy to agree.

We were seated at a comfortable table as many heads turned to see Hutt, the waiter was elegantly attentive, the lights were low, the hum of other diners barely noticeable, but as we settled into our cocktail conversation, I noticed Maureen Forrester two tables away. A palpable star in her own operatic sphere, she had an ego to match her talent. The two must surely have known of each other's presence, but neither seemed willing to acknowledge this. Hutt proceeded to sample many 'cathedrals' of drink, dropping ripe epigrams with casual ease as I tried hastily to record these in my pocket book like some latter-day Boswell to his well-oiled Samuel Johnson. I was, of course, working on his biography at the time.

The evening drew to a close, and when I had recovered from the pecuniary damage, I wondered aloud, 'Wasn't that Maureen Forrester?'

'Yes,' he replied with a hint of cold steel in the voice. 'She never seems to notice me. The last time we bumped into each other, she pretended she hadn't recognized me without her glasses.'

(Did she wear glasses? In public?)

Well, it seemed that Hutt could play her at her own game. The two were ships that would pass each other without so much as a little reciprocal semaphore.

There is no denying that Hutt is a star - on stages around the country, at Vancouver Airport where he was once greeted by half a dozen tapdancers in black bow-ties doing a number outside the baggage pickup, in the House of Commons where he has received official recognition by the Speaker of the House, or at Rideau Hall where he has been fêted by the Governor General for his services to theatre.

With friends, there is no ego. He is famous for his thoughtfulness and generosity, for he often goes to extraordinary lengths to please friends. The late Amelia Hall recounted how Hutt had shown great sensitivity to her aged, ailing mother one summer. Millie Hall and Hutt had been co-starring in a program of readings at the Guelph Summer Festival, but Mrs. Hall, in the throes of a deepening malady, was too ill to venture out of the Queen's Hotel. When Hutt appeared at the room to escort Millie to the show and bade the old lady goodbye, he noticed the wistful longing and loneliness in her eyes. He returned to his own room and fetched her a picture book with which to occupy her time, then said goodbye again.

On the highway, he suddenly blurted out: 'Oh, dammit! Let's take her!'

Dressing quickly, the old lady was white with excitement, and at the post-show party, she sat like Queen Victoria, beaming with regal pleasure. At her hotel door, she embraced Hutt: 'Oh, Bill, I do love you!'

'I love you too, Bill,' chimed in Millie, embracing him tightly as her blonde wig fell off.

I was present at his home one afternoon when Maggie Smith was astounded to learn that he had driven nine hours to see old friends in New York for a weekend.

'Bill, you are not a well person,' she gasped, utterly aghast, her famous nasal tone sending him into laughter. 'You are not a well person - driving nine hours to New York for a weekend. In England, if we drive nine hours, we run out of country!'

Civilities and social rituals count for something in his world. And as a performer, too, he expects correct manners, even though he pretends regret that some directors treat him with excessive deference. 'People don't direct me anymore,' he says with pseudo-wistfulness. Then he chuckles mockingly.

His much-heralded return to Stratford in 1993 was briefly marred by an unfortunate incident with a guest director who recklessly courted Hutt's displeasure by unmitigated rudeness in front of the entire company. Questioning the logic of a piece of blocking, Hutt was cut short and scolded as if he were a congenital idiot. He paused, then said slowly but firmly, 'I'm going to take a fifteen-minute break now' and simply walked off the stage.

His professional candour can be intimidating, even as it is bracingly accurate. When honoured with the Toronto Drama Bench Award in 1988, he succinctly summarized his attitude toward Stratford's various artistic directors: 'Guthrie gave the festival its inspiration, Langham its style, Gascon its lust, Robin Phillips its soul, John Hirsch its deficit, and John Neville took it away.' Nobody else could have been as pithy or as fortright.

Another candid moment occurred last season. Asked to do *Long Day's Journey into Night*, which was to be designed by Astrid Janson who has a brilliant, if sometimes extravagant imagination, he remarked pointedly, 'I don't want to be in this play looking as if it's taking place inside a bleeding lung.'

The consumptive Edmund Tyrone notwithstanding, there was no bleeding lung - but an austere middle-class New England summer house on stage.

He often stands on ceremony and has every right to do so, but there is often a sweet reason for the grand posture. When he directed *Gaslight* for Christopher Newton at Theatre Calgary in 1968, he made rather large demands. He didn't expect money (except from the Canada Council), but he demanded first-class airfare and hotel accommodation - which placed a heavy strain on the budget. But he was characteristically generous in turn with his own time, effort, and hospitality. He invited Board members for drinks in his suite at the Palliser, and played up the glamorous image of a star for all it was worth.

'His showing-off is a bit old-fashioned, but it's done out of a great sweetness,' commented Christopher Newton. 'This is like: I've set myself a goal and I've got it, so I must let other people know that I'm here for the benefit of everybody else. At the same time he was being grand for a strange kind of reason - to support people in the theatre. There's an old-time star in Bill, which is quite wonderful.'

Over twenty years later, Newton was delighted to have Hutt lend his considerable experience to the Shaw Festival company for two seasons, and even considered his request for three days off for a seventieth birthday celebration - 'The first to get back to Stratford, the second to get pissed, and the third to get over the hangover.' Well, Newton forgot the arrangement but compensated with a huge bash at the Prince of Wales Hotel, at which Peter Hutt made a hysterically funny speech and Newton a very gracious one.

He likes the privileges and embellishments of status, but he is unfailingly respectful, in turn, of a colleague's genius. He is unstinting in praise of others: Jason Robards is called 'such an uncompromising performer'; Martha Henry 'can do anything' on stage; Sheila McCarthy is 'enormously responsive'; Brent Carver is 'probably the most achingly vulnerable actor that I know.'

Nor is he inclined to stifle his public displays of approval. When Maggie Smith opened as an ivory Queen of the Nile in Phillips' surprisingly ascetic production of *Antony and Cleopatra*, he accorded her a standing ovation. Zoe Caldwell, herself a Cleopatra of great note in 1967, remarked cattily: 'Why, Bill, you were the only one standing!' To which he shot back: 'I always stand in the presence of greatness.'

And he did again - for Brent Carver in *Kiss of the Spider Woman* -and on other occasions accorded generous ovations to Vanessa Redgrave in *Orpheus Descending* and to Christopher Plummer in *No Man's Land*. These were cases of sheer joy at fellow-artists' transcendental successes.

The Plummer experience turned into a warm reunion for the two men who have not acted opposite each other in decades. The brilliant Plummer thrives on competition, which Hutt no longer needs as a spur to his ego. At drinks after the show, in which Hutt found his colleague to be 'startlingly wonderful' as Spooner, the two talked of many things, but through all the charming camaraderie, Plummer remained coyly competitive - *about the future!*

'When are you coming back to Stratford?' Hutt asked, knowing that his colleague had been talked to, coaxed, and endlessly wooed about returning to the site of much of his early glory.

'Well, I don't know, baby,' Plummer replied. 'I don't know about next year, because it's your seventy-fifth birthday and this book's coming out and all that!'

He said this with a chuckle, but there was a coy hint about the limelight he wasn't prepared to yield to anyone else.

Hutt's own ego is tremendous - and severely irritating to some colleagues - but assured of his position in the very forefront of classical actors on this continent, he has put aside unseemly competitiveness. Instead of being the lordly star who pushes the ensemble out of his light on stage, or instead of acting like part of a bureaucratic hierarchy - he is Consultant to the current Artistic Director, but this is largely an honorary position - Hutt prefers to adopt other personae. Sometimes these can be interesting performances in themselves.

During one of our recent long, lively taping sessions, he was in a particularly mellow mood, revelling quietly in his role as benevolently reflective memoirist. The stalled, formerly stellar career of an old, hard-drinking rival was lamented - not pompously or with condescension, but with sincere regret at the unfulfilled potential. Kate Reid's decline and passing were mourned for the unbridled waste of genuine talent. The 'glory' that was Max Helpmann, the 'zest' that was in Jean Gascon, the 'enormous promise' of Elliott Hayes all cast sombre shadows over the conversation. Old feuds and unpleasantries were mere residues in the alembick of a forgiving mind. John Hirsch, whom he had once mocked as 'a contradiction in sperms,' was now exalted. Time was when Hutt, wounded by Hirsch's insulting offers of inferior roles, sat on his long porch, sipping martinis, listening to some distant explosion caused by workers on a building project. 'Ah, a blast for another bomb in the theatre!' he gloated.

But now Hirsch, dead from Aids, was no longer the paranoid Machiavelli. 'He was very good at the dark stuff and very good at the Chekhov. I remember him doing a production of *Andorra* which was frightening. I was *in* it and it frightened me. I loved his passion. He didn't have the sense of love that Gascon had - the sense of camaraderie. And that was quite understandable in view of Hirsch's early life. God, that would sear anybody! After seeing *Schindler's List*, I now have to think in terms of John Hirsch's background more seriously than, perhaps, I did before. No wonder the joke went around that his forest of Arden was really the forest of Auschwitz. He had his vision, and things were dark, but he had passion. And God knows, Canadians are not known for their passion.'

Did he effect some sort of reconciliation with Hirsch after their Stratford falling-out?

'There wasn't much time to do that, darling. He died too soon.'

But melancholy regret was duly put aside in the quickening memories of sunnier topics. On Robin Phillips - 'Robin loves to talk, but it is always fascinating, *always* you will get something out of it if you listen.' On Christopher Newton - 'The best director of Shaw I've ever seen.' On Martha Henry - 'Like a conductor, she's got the whole score in her head before the rehearsal even begins.' On the young company he directed at Banff - 'The dear children gave me a beautiful attaché case as a present. The old one was just abominable.'

It was crystal clear that he had put away false pride, and was enjoying the memories of a career that has been well honoured in the main. 'I'm quite happy with the adoration I get and have got. My country has been good to me. And the fans in this country have been good to me - loyal and caring.'

He is a bright, particular star who is loved for his lustre.

SOME RECENT REVIEWS

SOME RECENT REVIEWS

HENRY VIII

'William Hutt's Wolsey...is a subtle, smiling villain. Tall and initially ascetic-looking, Hutt differs from our traditional idea of the fleshy Cardinal, drawn from contemporary portraits and the famous Orson Welles performance in the movie version...But Hutt slowly reveals the true nature of this seemingly lofty churchman.'
(Robert Crew, *The Toronto Star*, May 1986)

'...Hutt glides onto the stage as the power-brokering Wolsey and lowers himself onto a 16th-Century armchair, with his right hand (the one with the episcopal ring on it) out in space at just the right height off the floor for some supplicant to kneel and kiss it. It is hard to know who is craftier, Hutt or Wolsey, the way he extends that hand one way and disingenuously looks the other.'
(Lawrence DeVine, *Detroit Free Press*, May 1986)

'...the redoubtable Hutt...accepted the audience's welcome with royal grace and treated viewers to one of his vintage specialties: the oily hypocrite.....tall, gaunt body in brilliant red robes, a butter-melting smile on his face, mellifluous lies tumbling from his lips, his finger making tiny inveigling circles, as if inviting the many to challenge or disprove him.'
(Ray Conlogue, *The Globe and Mail*, May 1986)

A MAN FOR ALL SEASONS

'Playing a man torn between his king and the dictates of his own conscience, Hutt gives a masterly performance. But in the play's latter half, when More is imprisoned and facing certain death, Bolt's script becomes abstract and intellectual, and Hutt's approach turns too cool.'
(John Bemrose, *Maclean's*, August 1986)

'Of recent years Hutt seems to have largely abandoned the internal interrogation that actors must undergo when they do their best work. His unmatchable technique has become, like virtue, its own reward. Increasingly it is in the service of a generalized performance, and a generalized character.'
(Ray Conlogue, *The Globe and Mail*, July 1986)

'Hutt is literally tremendous....Here and there are moments in his interpretation which one feels may just possibly not be quite right, but he is so tremendous - that voice, that force, that precision of movement, that power of absolute stillness - that even when his rightness is in doubt, it doesn't matter, any more than it matters whether a lightning storm is right.'
(Doug Bale, *The London Free Press*, July 1986)

KING LEAR

'Hutt, who's played the title role in two previous productions, had always wanted to play Lear under Phillips' direction....For Hutt, it's not a question of third time lucky. It's third time unforgettable.'
(Barbara Cook, *The Ottawa Citizen*, June 1988)

'*Lear* is built around the venerable William Hutt, who arguably is Canada's finest actor, and certainly one of the finest in the English-speaking theater. This is the third *Lear* of Hutt's long career, and surely it is the most unique - a powerful, wonderfully controlled performance that makes us feel that we are meeting this familiar character for the first time.'
(Edward Hayman, *Detroit News*, June 1988)

'The dignity and nobility that Hutt's Lear ultimately achieves is hard won; the journey is both painful and shattering yet tightly drawn every step of the way by Hutt and Phillips.'
(Robert Crew, *The Toronto Star*, June 1988)

'Hutt can roar with the best of them. His performance, however, owes nothing to the rodomontade preferred in the past nor to the existential ruminations favored more recently. To this tragedy...he brings heart-breaking humanity. By play's end...all of us at the opening performance were in a state of stunned, tearful collapse.'
(Terry Doran, *Buffalo News*, June 1988)

'Through William Hutt's eloquently constrained and deeply moving portrait, we see not so much a man wrestling with elemental forces as a man reduced in every conceivable way by the sad, yet inevitable, infirmities of his own mortality.'
(Robert Reid, *Kitchener-Waterloo Record*, June 1988)

'The quiet buzzing tone of madness is acknowledged in Hutt's heart-breaking delivery of the lines "let me not be mad," quiet, pleading with unseen gods.'
(Ray Conlogue, *The Globe and Mail*, June 1988)

'The storm scene is daringly done: there is no roaring defiance of the elements from Lear here. Instead, while the thunder rages and the lightning cracks, an old man feebly trudges across the barren moor, stick beating a smothered tattoo on the ground, his voice and by implication his majesty shattered.'
(Jamie Portman, *Southam News*, June 1988)

THE MAN WHO CAME TO DINNER

'The role of Whiteside literally sits at the centre, so whatever is Falstaffian about the character (his portly size, massive self-indulgence in food and caprice, his roguishness and childishness) has to be conveyed rhetorically and by physical effects chiefly from the neck up. Hitting his consonants with sharp precision ("If you Do, I'll sPiT righT in your eye!"), and brandishing an elegant cigarette-holder as if to the manner born, he was the very image of elegant tyranny in his blue velvet smoking jacket and loud red tie. ...Whiteside can be played through the teeth, which is what Hutt did with relish. His comments came with icy composure, hitting his palate and clicking against his teeth. ...But it was not all dental virtuosity. Turning on his nurse for her gentle admonition against his eating pecan butternut fudge, he first pinned her with a merciless insult before licking his fingers. And it was hilarious because of the structured composure and timing.'
(Keith Garebian, *Theatrum*, May 1989)

MAN AND SUPERMAN

'In the balance is William Hutt's magnificent, witty Roebuck Ramsden, his first role with the Shaw Festival. It is a supporting role, a stock figure of the pompous parent, but Hutt gives him worlds of interior life and rich self-satisfaction.'
(Ray Conlogue, *The Globe and Mail*, May 1989)

'His is a performance of style and detail; few people can give a scene a lift in the way Hutt does with just a little pause, the sight hesitation over a name or sudden laugh.'
(Robert Crew, *The Toronto Star*, May 1989)

'Most formidable is William Hutt as the Commander. He is a raffish Falstaff who sneaks out of heaven for a bit of fun. To see Hutt, with a huge wig cascading down his back, inform Juan with sincere concern that he should liven up his speeches with an anecdote or two, is to see the picture of the loveable Philistine.'
(Ray Conlogue, *The Globe and Mail*, July 1989)

TRELAWNY OF THE 'WELLS'

'At first, Hutt's Sir William is a brittle, domineering old grouch who hides a tyrannical streak behind a concern for appropriate behavior. He walks as if he had a board stuck down the back of his jacket, a stiffness that makes for at least one wonderfully deliberate comic double take. It is in the third act, however, that Hutt truly shines....Obviously hurt by his grandson's flight, Sir William cracks ever so slightly, and Hutt, hands shaking, voice tentative, reveals that under that stiff surface lies the frustrated soul of an actor....Hutt's carefully controlled performance makes it the evening's most absorbing moment, a quick peek into the soul of a man who, until then, did not seem to have one.'
(Chris Dafoe, *The Globe and Mail*, August 1989)

'William Hutt's old authoritarian is beautiful: frail of body, stern of tongue, generous of spirit.'
(Robert Cushman, *The Globe and Mail*, May 1990)

'This veteran actor, savoring every crotchety nuance of speech, every pained twitch of the eyebrow, brings the judge to formidable life.'
(Jamie Portman, *Southam News*, August 1989)

THE WALTZ OF THE TOREADORS

'Hutt is idiosyncratic, at times sharply focussed, at others getting away with trickery rather than true exploration of character. His St. Pé is bitter, cynical, and most of all, small. His statement that "I can't make people suffer" sounds like a lame excuse rather than a moral stance.'
(Robert Crew, *The Toronto Star*, May 1990)

'If Mr. Hutt's general seems an unfinished character study, it may well be due to the production in which he is trapped. He does have some fine moments of cutting wit, others equally fine when the general shows how self-delusion can march hand-in-hand with self-awareness....Mr. Hutt knows how to give edge to a humorous phrase and to seek out the melancholy in the general's nature - the rueful realization of a long life unfulfilled. But his character's extended emotional breakdown at the very end of performance topples the play into sentimentality.'
(Jamie Portman, *Southam News*, May 1990)

'The General is a buffoon who suffers, and we cannot get at the suffering except through the buffoonery. William Hutt is too old for the role and would not have been right even when younger. He is a gallant actor - in both senses: brave and courteous - and he won all hearts at the curtain call. His technique...remains impeccable: give him an ironic aside and he will time and dispatch it with perfect finesse. But most of the time, his distinction works against him. Vulgarity and bluster are not in him; his balloon arrives on stage already punctured.'
(Robert Cushman, *The Globe and Mail*, May 1990)

THE COCKTAIL HOUR

'William Hutt takes command of the stage instantly, delightful as the domineering, opinonated raconteur booming instruction, indulging in groanworthy bouts of self-pity, doing much with little, and generally recalling past glories with familiar polish.'
(Geoff Chapman, *The Toronto Star*, November 1990)

'William Hutt's Bradley, caught in a blue blazer that displays his admirable physique and petty vanity, rolls forward through the action on a mellow and lugubrious voice....he recognizes that Bradley is merely an emblem of a certain lifestyle rather than a carefully drawn character. But he displays his inimitable command of the comic pause and the final syllable delivered at exactly the right moment, generating far more laughter with the role than I recall from its original New York production.'
(Ray Conlogue, *The Globe and Mail*, November 1990)

THE DINING ROOM

'...Hutt, in addition to playing one of the young guests at the afore-mentioned birthday bash, is more apt as a stern patriarch who complains to the servant about a seed in his morning juice and as a cranky capitalist dispensing advice to his grandson.'
(Vit Wagner, *The Toronto Star*, November 1992)

'Hutt is brilliant in his chameleon-like performance, changing from aging patriarch to petulant five year-old easily and convincingly.'
(Michelle McColm, *Spotlight Magazine*, November 1992)

'With so many captivating scenes, it's difficult to single out; but the sketch where William Hutt as the aging father talks over his funeral arrangements with his son (Peter Hutt) is perhaps the most memorable.'
(Fred Browning, *Courier Press*, November 1992)

A CHRISTMAS CAROL

'His transformation from tight-lipped and tight-fisted to open-hearted and open-handed is beautifully executed. He can certainly be forgiven for being no singer; his singing parts manage to be reasonably melodious in any case.'
(Sheila Martindale, *Scene*, January 1993)

'...Hutt doesn't so much walk through his current part as dance lightly across its surface, scarcely leaving a footprint.'
(Doug Bale, *The London Free Press*, December 1992)

THE STILLBORN LOVER

'[Hutt's] gradual emergence as the gentle and moral Harry is the compelling centrepiece the production needs.'
(Vit Wagner, *The Toronto Star*, April 1993)

'Raymond is a broken man and Hutt is absolutely superb in the role.'
(Jennifer Hale, *The Gazette* (UWO), March 1993)

'William Hutt gently unravels Harry Raymond for us, making us see the pain of his struggle, his attempts to protect the wife he still loves and the daughter who doesn't quite understand him.'
(Jeffrey Canton, *Now*, April 1993)

THE IMAGINARY INVALID

'The outward tools of his craft are evident enough - the quaver in the voice, the richness of the body language, a marvellously mobile face which in rapid succession can register childlike delight, towering rage, absurd self-pity, eye-rolling terror. Yet he goes far beyond a collection of mere mannerisms here. What Hutt delivers is the portrait of an obsession, insulated from the realities of his existence by a fortress-like self-absorption, yet undermined by his character's own vulnerability. (Jamie Portman, *The London Free Press*, August 1993)

'Hutt is center-stage full time. He's the whole show, like Washington, Jefferson, Lincoln and Roosevelt merged into one. When he actually moves, that's a plus. A playgoer had better like Hutt going in this time, because the production is heavy going. (Lawrence Devine, *Detroit Free Press*, August 1993)

LOVE LETTERS

'Hutt...treated his role too ironically....While less distracting initially, over the course of the evening, Hutt's air of knowingness and slightly amused detachment got in the way of my response...' (Gaile MacGregor, *The Plus*, November 1993)

HAMLET

'Several key parts are taken by younger members of the company. They do a passable job, but when old Stratford hands Douglas Rain (Polonius) and Hutt (the First Gravedigger) launch into their lines, it is like watching Wayne Gretzky and Mario Lemieux stickhandle effortlessly through a pack of minor leaguers.' (John Bemrose, *Maclean's*, June 1994)

'I would like to have seen more acting from William Hutt as the Ghost of Hamlet's father, which he plays in a monotone - a mighty pipe organ held to one note - although Hutt's no-contact "hug" with Hamlet as he bids him "adieu, adieu, adieu" is chillingly effective; he also turns in a typically skilled job doubling as the comic First Gravedigger.'
(H.J. Kirchhoff, *The Globe and Mail*, June 1994)

'William Hutt manages to be both spectral and regal as the ghost of Hamlet's father, and later transforms himself into a wheezing comic delight in the role of the First Gravedigger.'
(Jamie Portman, *The Ottawa Citizen*, June 1994)

LONG DAY'S JOURNEY INTO NIGHT

'There is a scene near the end of the Stratford Festival's production of *Long Day's Journey into Night* that is, simply, magnificent theatre. Stratford veteran William Hutt - playing the retired actor James Tyrone - tells his son Edmund (Tom McCamus) the story of his impoverished boyhood, when he was forced to quit school and work in a factory. Then he goes on to recall how he became an actor - and detroyed his talent by spending his best years in a commercially successful but artistically inferior play. Hutt delivers his lines with such clarity and luminous simplicity that, during a recent performance, the 500-seat Tom Patterson Theatre became completely silent - except for the faint snuffling of people struggling to hold back tears. It is one of those rare, timeless moments when a great performer combines with a great play to catch something of life's elusive mystery.'
(John Bemrose, *Maclean's*, June 1994)

'Mr. Hutt completely sidesteps the bombast that usually colors James Tyrone and has him carrying on with the leftover arrogance of a matinée idol. What emerges in the actor's performance instead is the emptiness of a man who knows he has spoiled his life and desperately needs to make some sense of the wreckage. Jack Lemmon, who played the role in the hyped-up 1986 Broadway revival, directed by Jonathan Miller, found the character so solid, so immovable, he said it was like playing an oak tree. Mr. Hutt, to the contrary, seems to be doing everything in his power

to be accommodating. When the old angers seize him anyway, the effect is doubly powerful.'
(David Richards, *The New York Times*, June 1994)

CHRONOLOGY: WILLIAM HUTT

CHRONOLOGY: WILLIAM HUTT

Chronological table of parts, assignments, and productions*
1948
  Mark Shawn Players,   *Claudia*   David
  Bracebridge   *Theatre*   Michael Gosselyn
                       Night Must Fall   Dan
                       Separate Rooms   Jim Stackhouse
                       The Vinegar Tree   Max Lawrence
1949
  Tour   *Arsenic and Old Lace* Mortimer
1950
  Niagara Falls   *No Time for Comedy* Gaylord Easterbrook
  Summer Theatre   *Harvey*   Dr. William Chumley
                       Night Must Fall   Dan
                       Private Lives   Elyot
                       Angel Street   Mr. Manningham

1951
  Niagara Falls   *Hay Fever*   Richard Greatham
  Summer Theatre   *A Streetcar Named
                         Desire*   Mitch
                         The Little Foxes   Uncle Ben
                         French Without Tears Naval Commander

                         Our Town   Simon Stimson
                         Present Laughter   Gary Essendene
                         Charley's Aunt   Sir Fancourt
                                                 Babberley
                         *The Importance
                         of Being Earnest*   Rev. Chasuble
                         Gramercy Park   Ambulance Driver
                         *The Petrified
                         Forest*   Jackie
1952
  Niagara Falls   *The Rose Tattoo*   Salesman
  Summer Theatre   *Nina*   M. Redon-LaMur
  Canadian Reper-   *Captain Carvallo*   Captain Carvallo
  tory Theatre,   *The Happiest Days
  Ottawa   of Your Life*   Dick Tassell
                         The Gioconda Smile   Henry Hutton
                         Castle in the Air   Earl of Locharne
                         *Grand National
                         Night*   Gerald Coates
                         The Miser   Harpagon
                         The Three Sisters   Vershinin
                         Nina   The Lover
                         *The Lady's Not
                         For Burning*   Edward Tappercoom

1953

CRT, Ottawa	*The Seventh Veil*	Nicholas Cunningham
	Victoria Regina	Benjamin Disraeli
Stratford	*Richard III*	Sir James Blunt/Sir
Festival, Ontario		Robert Brakenbury
	All's Well That Ends Well	Minister of State
CRT, Ottawa	*The Deep Blue Sea*	William Collyer
	The Biggest Thief in Town	Bert Hutchins
	Relative Values	Crestwell
	Tartuffe	3rd Actor/Tartuffe
	Mr. Bolfry	Mr. McCrimmon
	Misalliance	Lord Summerhays

1954

CRT, Ottawa	*The Noble Spaniard*	Duke of Hermanos
	The Country Girl	Bernie Dodd
	The Holly and the Ivy	David Paterson
	The Mask and the Face	Count Mario Grazia
	Someone at the Door	Price
	The Late Edwina Black	Gregory Black
	See How They Run	The Intruder
Stratford	*Measure for Measure*	Froth
Festival, Ontario	*The Taming of the Shrew*	Hortensio
	Oedipus Rex	Chorus Leader
Canadian Players tour	*Saint Joan*	Archbishop/Warwick/ de Courcelles
Crest Theatre	*Diary of a Scoundrel*	Gloumov

1955
   Stratford | *Julius Caesar* | Cinna/Ligarius
| *Oedipus Rex* | Chorus Leader

Stratford Festival, Ontario	*Julius Caesar* *Oedipus Rex* *The Merchant of* *Venice*	Cinna/Ligarius Chorus Leader Old Gobbo
Canadian Players	*Macbeth*	Macbeth
1956		
Royal Alexandra Theatre, Toronto	*Tamburlaine the* *Great*	Techelles
Winter Garden, New York	*Tamburlaine the* *Great*	Techelles
Stratford Festival, Ontario	*Henry V*	Archbishop of Canterbury
	The Merry Wives *of Windsor*	Ford
(Film)	*Oedipus Rex*	Chorus Leader
Assembly Hall, Edinburgh	*Oedipus Rex* *Henry V*	Chorus Leader Archbishop of Canterbury
CBC-TV	*The Public Prosecutor*	title-role
1956-57		
Canadian Players tour	*Hamlet* *Peer Gynt*	Hamlet Button Moulder/ Troll King
1957		
Stratford, Ontario	*Hamlet*	Polonius
Phoenix Theatre, New York	*Mary Stuart* *The Makropoulos* *Secret*	Earl of Shrewsbury Dr. Kolonaty
1958		
Stratford, Ontario	*Henry IV, Part One* *Much Ado About* *Nothing*	Worcester Don Pedro
CBC-TV	*Diary of a Scoundrel*	Gloumov
CBC-TV	*A Month in the* *Country*	Rakitin
Hofstra College	*Hamlet*	Hamlet

1959
(Television)	*The Greatest Man in the World*	
CBC-TV	*Ivanov*	Ivanov
Bristol Old Vic	*Long Day's Journey Into Night*	James Tyrone, Sr.
CBC-TV	*The Cocktail Party*	Edward Chamberlayne
Stratford, Ontario	*As You Like It*	Jaques
	Othello	Lodovico

1960
Salisbury Playhouse	*The Truth about Billy Newton*	William Newton
London	*Waiting in the Wings*	Alan Bennet
(Television)	*Macbeth*	Ross
BBC-TV	*Parasol*	Anatol
(Film)	*There Was a Crooked Man*	U.S. Secretary of State

1961-62
U.S. tour	*Sail Away*	Lawford Craig
Canadian Players tour	*King Lear*	King Lear
	The Lady's Not For Burning	Thomas Mendip
CBC-TV	*Village Wooing*	'A'

1962
CBC-TV	*The Prisoner*	Interrogator
Stratford, Ontario	*Macbeth*	Banquo
	The Tempest	Prospero
	Cyrano de Bergerac	Carbon de Castel
(Television)	*Cyrano de Bergerac*	Carbon de Castel
CBC-TV	*The Offshore Island*	

1963
(Television)	*The Affliction of Love*	
Stratford, Ontario	*Troilus and Cressida*	Pandarus
	Cyrano de Bergerac	Carbon de Castel
	Timon of Athens	Alcibiades

1963-64
  Canadian Players   *Private Lives*   Elyot
  tour   *Masterpieces of*
        Comedy   assorted roles
1964
  CBC-TV   *Uncle Vanya*   Vanya
  Stratford Festival   *Love's Labour's Lost*   Don Armado
  at Chichester   *Le Bourgeois*
        Gentilhomme   Dorante
        Timon of Athens   Alcibiades
  Stratford, Ontario   *Richard II*   Richard II
        Le Bourgeois
        Gentilhomme   Dorante
        The Country Wife   Sparkish
  New York   *Tiny Alice*   Lawyer
  CBC-TV   *The Magician of*
        Lublin   Rabbi
1965
  Stratford, Ontario   *Falstaff (Henry IV*
        Part Two)   Shallow
        Julius Caesar   Marcus Brutus
        The Cherry Orchard   Leonid Gaev
  Manitoba Theatre   *The Importance of*
  Centre   *Being Earnest*   John Worthing
        Andorra   Can, the teacher
1966
  Manitoba T.C.   *Nicholas Romanov*   Grand Duke Michael
  Stratford, Ontario   *Henry V*   Chorus
        Henry VI   Warwick
        The Last of the Tsars   Grand Duke Michael
1967
  (Television)   *Henry V*   Chorus
  Stratford Festival   *The Government*
  and tour   *Inspector*   Khlestakov
        Twelfth Night   Feste
  Stratford, Ontario   *Richard III*   Clarence
        Antony and
        Cleopatra   Enobarbus
  (Film)   *The Fixer*   Tsar

1968
   Stratford, Ontario   *Tartuffe*   Tartuffe
                             The Seagull   Trigorin
                             Waiting for Godot   (director)
   Theatre Calgary   *Gaslight*   (director)
   Lincoln Centre, N.Y.   *Saint Joan*   Warwick
1969
   Theatre Toronto   *Edward II*   Edward II
   CBC-TV   *Conversation with*
                             Coffee   (readings)
   Stratford, Ontario   *The Alchemist*   Sir Epicure Mammon
                             Measure for Measure   Duke Vincentio
                             Tartuffe   Tartuffe
1970
   Leatherhead, U.K.   *Caesar and Cleopatra*   Caesar
   Chichester Festival   *The Alchemist*   Sir Epicure Mammon
                             Vivat! Vivat! Regina!   Cardinal of
                                                  Lorraine
                             Peer Gynt   Ingrid's Father
   National Arts
   Centre, Ottawa   *Tartuffe*   Tartuffe
   CBC-TV   *Becket: Motives of*
                             the Murder   King Henry II
1971
   Stratford, Ontario   *Much Ado About*
                             Nothing   (director)
                             Volpone   Volpone
1972
   Stratford, Ontario   *As You Like It*   (director)
                             King Lear   King Lear
                             Mark   (director)
   CBC-TV   *Stratford - Twenty*
                             Years Young   (narrator)

1973
  European tour   *King Lear*   King Lear
  Stratford, Ontario   *A Month in the*
                         Country   (director)
                         The Marriage
                         Brokers   (director)
1974
  Australian tour   *The Imaginary*
                         Invalid   Argan
  Stratford, Ontario   *The Imaginary*
                         Invalid   Argan
                         Love's Labour's Lost Don Armado
  (Television)   *The National Dream* Sir John A.
                                              Macdonald
1975
  Stratford, Ontario   *Saint Joan*   (director)
                         Measure for Measure Duke Vincentio
                         Trumpets and Drums Captain Brazen
                         Oscar Remembered   (director)
                         The Importance of
                         Being Earnest   Lady Bracknell
  (Television)   *The First Night of*
                         'Pygmalion'   Bernard Shaw
1976
  Stratford, Ontario   *Hamlet*   (co-director)
                         The Tempest   Prospero/(co-director)
                         The Importance of
                         Being Earnest   Lady Bracknell
                         Measure for Measure Duke Vincentio
                         Three Sisters   Chebutykin
  Theatre London   *Candida*   (director)
1977
  Theatre London   *Long Day's Journey*
                         Into Night   James Tyrone, Sr.
  Stratford, Ontario   *All's Well That*
                         Ends Well   King of France
                         Ghosts   Pastor Manders
                         Hay Fever   David Bliss

1978
    Theatre London   *Twelfth Night*   (director)
    Stratford, Ontario   *The Merry Wives*
                           of Windsor   Falstaff
                           Uncle Vanya   Ivan Petrovich
                           Titus Andronicus   Titus Andronicus
    Theatre London   *Kiss Me, Kate*   (director)
1979
    Theatre London   *Rope*   (director)
                           Oscar Remembered   (director)
                           John A.--Himself!   John A. Macdonald
                           Litte Mary Sunshine   (director)
                           The Music of Words
                           in Words and Music   (co-director)
    Stratford, Ontario   *The Importance of*
                           Being Earnest   Lady Bracknell
                           The Woman   Nestor
                           King Lear   Fool
    Theatre London   *The Hollow Crown*
1980
    Theatre London   *Equus*   Martin Dysart
                           The Indian Wants
                           the Bronx   (director)
    Stratford, Ontario   *Twelfth Night*   Feste
                           Titus Andronicus   Titus Andronicus
                           Much Ado About
                           Nothing   Leonato
                           The Seagull   Dr. Dorn
                           King Lear   Fool
                           Long Day's Journey
                           Into Night   James Tyrone, Sr.
1981
    Stratford, Ontario   *The Visit*   Anton Schill
    (Film)   *The Wars*   Mr. Ross
    (Film)   *Models*
1982
    NBC-TV   *The Elephant Man*   Bishop
    Vancouver Playhouse   *The Dresser*   Sir

1983
    Vancouver Playhouse *Mass Appeal*   Fr. Tim Fairley
    Grand Theatre,   *Timon of Athens*   Timon of Athens
    London, Ontario   *The Doctor's*
                Dilemma   Sir Ralph Bloom-
                            field Bonington
                Arsenic and Old Lace Abigail Brewster
1984
    Grand Theatre,   *Hamlet*   Claudius
    London, Ontario   *Dear Antoine*   Cravatar
    Vancouver   *A Man for All*
    Playhouse   *Seasons*   Sir Thomas More
                Clarence Darrow   Clarence Darrow
    NAC, Ottawa   *New World*   Bob
1985
    CentreStage, T.O.   *New World*   Bob
    Vancouver Playhouse *Who's Afraid of*
                Virginia Woolf?   George
1986
    Stratford, Ontario   *Henry VIII*   Wolsey
                A Man For All
                Seasons   Sir Thomas More
1987
    Stratford, Ontario   *The School for*
                Scandal   Sir Peter Teazle
                Much Ado About
                Nothing   Leonato
    Vancouver Playhouse *Master Class*   Zhdanov
1988
    (Television)   *Much Ado About*
                Nothing   Leonato
    Stratford, Ontario   *King Lear*   King Lear
    Theatre London   *The Man Who Came*
                To Dinner   Sheridan Whiteside

1990

Theatre London	*The Road to Mecca*	Marius Byleveld
Shaw Festival,	*Man and Superman*	Roebuck Ramsden
Niagara-on-the-Lake	*Trelawny of the 'Wells'*	Sir William Gower
Theatre London	*The Cocktail Hour*	Bradley

1991

Citadel Theatre, Edmonton	*The Cocktail Hour*	Bradley
Shaw Festival	*Trelawny of the 'Wells'*	Sir William Gower
	Waltz of the Toreadors	General St. Pé

1992

Banff	*Twelfth Night*	(director)
Citadel Theatre/ Manitoba T.C.	*Lend Me a Tenor*	Saunders
Theatre London	*The Dining Room*	Actor #1
	A Christmas Carol	Ebenezer Scrooge

1993

Theatre London	*The Stillborn Lover*	Harry Raymond
Stratford, Ontario	*The Imaginary Invalid*	Argan
Theatre London	*Love Letter*	Andrew Makepeace Ladd, III
	A Christmas Carol	Ebenezer Scrooge

1994

Stratford, Ontario	*Long Day's Journey Into Night*	James Tyrone, Sr.
	Hamlet	Ghost/First Gravedigger

* Archival records are incomplete, so in some cases certain roles and productions are unknown. This chronology lists only significant film and television credits, and has been compiled with the kind co-operation of John Connell, William Hutt, Lee Ramsay of the Metropolitan Toronto Reference Library, Nancy Sadek and Parvin Jahanpour of the University of Guelph Theatre Archives, and Leonard Belsher of The Grand Theatre.

INDEX

Agate, James, 23
Albee, Edward, 100
Alchemist, The, 5, 68, 96
Andorra, 157
Anglin, Ann, 96
Antony and Cleopatra, 156
Applebaum, Louis, 51
Armstrong, Pat, 97
Arsenic and Old Lace, 69, 136
As You Like It, 32, 107, 119
Askey, Maggie, 65
Atherton, Ted, 137, 140
Atienza, Edward, 144
Atkinson, Brooks, 32
Baker, Bob, 73
Ball, Michael, 95
Balsam, Martin, 3
Barnes, Clive, 36
Barrymore, John, 23
Bates, Alan, 57
Bawtree, Michael, 50-5

Bedford, Brian, 36, 38
Bernhardt, Sarah, 153
Berton, Pierre, 15
Blake, Mervyn, xiii, 80-2, 121-23, 144-45
Blendick, James, 56-9, 96, 149-50
Blythe, Domini, 73
Bochner, Lloyd, 30
Boyko, Christine, 22
Braithwaite, Lillian, 28
Brett, Jeremy, 152
Bridges, Beau, 5
Bridges, Jeff, 5
Brook, (Mr. and Mrs.) John F., 118
Brook, Pamela, 117-20
Budd, Barbara, 124-31
Burns, Martha, 46
Burton, Richard, 23, 153
Caldwell, Zoe, 31, 34, 57, 156
Campbell, Douglas, 30, 99, 145

Campbell, Graeme, 46, 129
Campbell, Mrs. Patrick, 153
Carnwath, Drew, 140
Carver, Brent, 42, 46, 156
Casson, Jane, 123
Chalmers, Floyd, 52
Charpentier, Gabriel, 50
Chekhov, Anton, xi, 17, 100
Cherry Orchard, The, 17, 33, 73
Chilcott, Barbara, 14
Christie, Agatha, 53
Christie, Robert, 30
Christmann, Mark, 140
Clark, Patrick, 137, 139
Clements, Sir John, 39
Clurman, Harold, 22
Cobb, David, 39
Cocteau, Jean, 28
Colicos, John, 31, 153
Collins, Patricia, 101-2
Congreve, William, 41
Connell, John, xiii, 3-12
Connell, Mila, 4
Cooper, Alec, 148
Coward, Sir Noel, xi, 28-9, 99, 100
Coyne, Susan, 112
Cusack, Cyril, 21
Dale, Jennifer, 73
Dare, Daphne, 40, 73
Darrow, 69-70
Davis, Donald, 14, 30
Davis, Murray, 14
Depardieu, Gérard36
Dining Room, The, 114
Dolha, Andrew, 140
Donaldson, Peter, 46, 112
Donkin, Eric, 96
Dover, Carol, 140
Easton, Richard, 30

Edward II, 114
Evans, Dame Edith, 7, 39
Every Inch A Lear, 84-5
Fabulous Baker Boys, The, 5
Famous Last Words, 13
Findley, Timothy, xi, 13-8, 23, 30, 40, 43, 102
Forrester, Maureen, 153-4
Frehner, Harry, 139
Galloway, Pat, 36, 69
Gardner, David, 14, 32, 81
Garebian, Keith, 19-49, 100, 151-8
Gascon, Jean, xii, 35, 36, 41, 96, 112, 145, 155, 157
Gaslight, 96-7, 155
Gerussi, Bruno, 30
Gielgud, Sir John, 28, 39, 99, 153
Gill, Robert, 14, 28, 118, 119
Gish, Dorothy, 29
Gish, Lillian, 3, 29
Gogol, Nikolai, 33, 100
Goldsmith, Oliver, 50
Good, Maurice, 73, 83-92
Gordon, Lewis, 73
Gordon, Ruth, 13
Government Inspector, The, 33, 58
Grand Inquisitor, The, 44
Guinness, Sir Alec, 20, 29
Guthrie, Sir Tyrone, 29, 30, 41, 46, 119, 138, 155
Hall, Amelia, 28, 29, 30, 52, 54, 154
Hamilton, Patricia, xiii, 132- 40
Hamlet, 45
Harron, Donald, 30
Hayes, Elliott, 157
Hayes, John, 54
Heeley, Desmond, 73
Heldt, Sharon, 140

Helpmann, Max, 157
Henry, Martha, 16, 24, 36, 38,
    45, 46, 96, 102, 112,
    129,135, 156, 158
Henry IV - Part Two, 17
Henry V, 112
Henry VIII, 78
Heyerdahl, Chris, 137, 140
Hirsch, John, 36, 41, 44, 145,
    155, 157-8
Hitch, Mary, 96
Hopkins, Bernard, 21, 73
House, Eric, 14, 30, 152-3
Howard, Sidney, 15
Hughes, Stuart, 112
Hurry, Leslie, 51
Hutt, Edward DeWitt, 26
Hutt, Mountain, 27
Hutt, Peter, 129, 156
Hutt, William, as director: 96- 7,
    118-9, 122-3, 125-7, 135-9;
    PARTS: Argan *(The Imaginary
    Invalid),* 36, 112; Lady
    Bracknell *(The Importance of
    Being Earnest),* 7-9, 42, 61-2,
    64-6; Chorus Leader *(Oedipus
    Rex),* 29; Clarence Darrow
    (Darrow), 69-70; Duke *(Meas-
    ure for Measure),* 37-9, 40;
    Enobarbus *(Antony and
    Cleopatra),* 31; Sir John
    Falstaff *(The Merry Wives of
    Windsor),* 73-9; Fool *(King
    Lear),* 43, 85-92; Ford *(The
    Merry Wives of Windsor),*
    31; Gaev *(The Cherry
    Orchard),* 17, 33-4; Hortensio
    (The Taming of the Shrew),
    29; Jaques *(As You Like It),* 32,
    107; Khlestakov *(The

Government Inspector), 33;
    Lear *(King Lear),* 6, 10-2, 40-
    1, 44, 68-9, 81-2, 144-5; Sir
    John A. Macdonald *(John A. -
    Himself!),* 15-6; Sir Epicure
    Mammon *(The Alchemist),* 5,
    37- 8; Grand Duke Michael
    (The Last of the Tsars), 54;
    Pandarus *(Troilus and Cressida),*
    32, 33; Polonius *(Hamlet),*
    32; Roebuck Ramsden *(Man
    and Superman),* 94-5; Harry
    Raymond *(The Stillborn
    Lover),* 16, 23-6, 104-5;
    Richard II *(Richard II),* 32-3;
    Shallow *(Henry IV),* 17;
    Tartuffe *(Tartuffe),* 35-6; Sir
    Peter Teazle *(The School for
    Scandal),* 41-2; Timon
    (Timon of Athens), 42-3; James
    Tyrone *(Long Day's Journey
    Into Night),* 46-9, 108, 111-2;
    Volpone *(Volpone),* 37
Hyland, Frances, 29, 30, 52,112
Ibsen, Henrik, xi
Imaginary Invalid, The, 36, 45,
    103, 112, 120
Importance of Being Earnest, The,
    7, 42, 65, 114
Jackson, Brian, 73
Janson, Astrid, 155
John A. - Himself!, xi, 15
Jonson, Ben, 32, 96
Kaye, Arden, 40
Kean, Edmund, 153
Kelly, Gene, 65
Kenyon, Joel, 52
Kerr, Walter, 29, 31, 36, 37-8
Kiley, Richard, 3
King, Charmion, 14, 28

King Lear, 9, 10, 22, 35, 40,   41, 44, 68, 69, 81-2, 145

Kinsolving, William, 51-2, 54

Kirchner, James, 140

Kiss Me, Kate, 72

Kiss of the Spider Woman, 156

Klugman, Jack, 3

Krystyan, Vieslav, 140

Langham, Michael, xii, 31, 32, 35, 41, 51-5, 57-8, 112, 147, 155

Lansbury, Angela, 65

Last of the Tsars, The, 50

Laughton, Charles, 114

Leblanc, Diana, 46, 110-12

Lepage, Robert, 136

LeSage, Jeanne, 139

Lockhart, Araby, 14

Long Day's Journey Into Night, 20, 45, 108, 111, 129, 155

Macbeth, 6

MacGregor, Barry, 69, 73, 74, 146-8

MacLennan, Cynthia, 76-7

MacMillan, Richard, 73

Makropoulos Secret, The, 30

Man and Superman, 94-5

Man Who Came To Dinner, The, 45

Maraden, Marti, 60-2

March, Fredric, 46

Mary Stuart, 30

Mason, James, 29

Massingham, Andrew, 137, 140

Matchmaker, The, 13

McCamus, Tom, 45, 46, 111

McCarthy, Sheila, 41, 156

McGarvin, Michael, 27

McGarvin, Reaveley, 27

Measure for Measure, 37, 40, 68, 129

Merry Wives of Windsor, The, 31, 72-9, 103

Millaire, Albert, xii, 112

Mirren, Helen, 39

Moiseiwitsch, Tanya, 36, 73

Molière, xi, 36, 100

Monette, Richard, 45, 106-9, 145

Morgan, Winston, 139

Moss, Peter, 23, 73-5, 79, 101-2

Much Ado About Nothing, 103, 109, 119, 123

Munro, Neil, 96

Murrell, John, xi

National Dream, The, 15

Needles, William, 30, 73

Neville, John, 39, 44, 69, 155

New World, xi, 41

Newton, Christopher, 44, 45, 93-7, 155-6, 158

Nicholas Romanov, 51-2, 54

No Man's Land, 156

Novick, Julius, 33

Odd Couple, The, 96

Oedipus Rex, 29, 30

Olivier, Sir Laurence (later Lord), 20, 22,   28, 36, 41-2, 46, 47, 61, 82, 100, 123

Ondine, 118-9

O'Neill, Eugene, xi, 100

Ormerod, John, 112

Orpheus Descending, 156

O'Toole, Peter, 28

Ouchi, Mieko, 140

Ouimette, Stephen, 16, 45

Ouzounian, Richard, 63-6

Palk, Nancy, 112

Papavs, Vicki, 137, 140

Patria II, 50

Pelletier, Denise, 112

Pennell, Nicholas, 8, 148
Pfeiffer, Michelle, 5
Phillips, Robin, xii, 9, 10-1, 13, 23,
    37, 38, 39, 40, 41, 42, 43, 44,
    46, 64, 69, 72, 81, 84, 88-91,
    112, 125, 129-30, 133-4, 148,
    155, 156, 158
Phipps, Jennifer, 16, 73
Pinero, Sir Arthur Wing, xi, 45,
    100
Planche, Valerie, 140
Plowright, Joan, 39
Plummer, Christopher, 29, 31,
    32, 39, 57, 99, 144, 156-7
Polley, Nora, 67-70
Pownall, Leon, 123
Private Lives, 40
Ragsdale, Robert C., 79, 113-4
Rain, Douglas, 30, 39-40, 99,
    112
Ralston, John, 140
Rathbone, Basil, 114
Redgrave, Sir Michael, 22, 23, 82
Redgrave, Vanessa, 156
Reid, Kate, 14, 157
Richard III, 20
Richardson, Ian, 39
Richardson, Sir Ralph, 47
Road to Mecca, The, 112
Robards, Jason, 3, 156
Roberts, Jean, 96
Robison, Ian, 140
Roux, Jean-Louis, 112
Saint Joan, 31, 122, 127
Savidge, Mary, 73, 79
Scarfe, Alan, 73
Schafer, Murray, 50
Schindler's List, 158
School for Scandal, The, 41, 44
Schultz, Albert, 112

Scofield, Paul, 31, 99
Scott, Barbara Ann, 126, 127
Sevareid, Eric, 12
Shakespeare, William, xi, 28, 100
Shatner, William, 29, 30
Shaw, George Bernard, xi, 28, 45
Shawn, Mark, 28
She Stoops To Conquer, 50
Shelley, Carole, 69
Shepherd, Elizabeth, 69
Sheridan, Richard Brinsley, 41
Sidney, Sylvia, 29
Silver, Phillip, 42, 43, 71-9
Silver Cord, The, 15
Simon, John, 23
Simpson, Denis, 42
Singing in the Rain, 65
Smith, Dame Maggie, 99, 154-5,
    156
Stillborn Lover, The, xi, 13,   16,
    23-4, 102, 148
Sutherland, Donald, 153
Tamburlaine the Great, 30
Taming of the Shrew, The, 29
Tandy, Jessica, 39, 46, 99, 129
Tartuffe, 120
Tempest, The, 127, 128, 148
Terry, Dame Ellen, 25
Theatre, 19
Thomas, Powys, 54, 69
Thorndike, Dame Sybil, 28
Timon of Athens, 42
Tiny Alice, 59
Tone, Franchot, 29
Troilus and Cressida, 32, 73
Turenne, Louis, 34
Twelfth Night, 135-40
Ustinov, Sir Peter, 10, 43, 84-9,
    90-1, 99
Valk, Frederick, 31, 99

Van Bridge, Tony, 54, 99
Waiting For Godot, 87
Waiting in the Wings, 29
Waltz of the Toreadors, The, 44, 112
Wardle, Irving, 9
Warner, David, 39
Wars, The, 13
Webster, William, 112
Well-Bred Muse, A, 19
Welsh, Kenneth, 96, 123
Whelan, Richard, 73
Whitehead, William, 15
Whittaker, Herbert, 32, 40, 98-
    100, 153
Whittaker's Theatricals, 153
Wilde, Oscar, xi
Wilder, Thornton, 13
William, David, 11, 35, 37, 44, 45,
    82, 144
William Hutt: A Theatre Portrait,
    19, 26
Wilson, Lynn, 35
Wood, Caroline Frances Havergal,
    26
Wood, Peter, 32
Wood, Tom, 73
Worth, Irene, 29, 39
Yeo, Leslie, 122